THE AU⌐

J IMMIE MACGREGOR is a gradu⌐
Art, and has been, among o⌐
engraver, potter, naturalist, labo⌐ _⌐⌐⌐er, author,
illustrator, and radio and television ⌐⌐⌐⌐er. He was deeply
involved in the early days of the folk music revival in Britain, and
remained in the forefront of that movement for more than twenty
years, becoming a household name through countless radio, concert
and television appearances. He has toured the length and breadth of
Britain many times, appearing in all kinds of venues from tiny folk
clubs to the country's great theatres and concert halls, and his songs
have taken him to Canada, Israel, the United States, Australia,
Belgium, Holland, France, New Zealand, Germany, Russia, Austria
and the Middle East.

Jimmie has made more than twenty long-playing albums, while
several of his own songs and tunes have been used by fellow
musicians, and he has composed and played theme music for radio
and television. He has won an award for voice-over commentary on
video, and his own highly successful daily programme, *Macgregor's
Gathering*, on BBC Radio Scotland, has been going for more than
seven years. The programme was granted a special prize by the Royal
Society for the Protection of Birds, for its significant contribution to
wildlife and conservation. Jimmie Macgregor has been made Scot of
the Year by two separate organisations. He is a life member of the
Scottish Wildlife Trust, and honorary vice-president of the Glasgow
branch of the Scottish Youth Hostels Association, and Scottish
Conservation Projects.

The BBC television series on which this book is mainly based is
the fifth in the *Macgregor's Scotland* series; the others are: *The West
Highland Way, The Moray Coast, Speyside and the Cairngorms* (Speyside
Way), *In the Footsteps of Bonnie Prince Charlie*, and *On the Outer Edge*
(remote Scottish islands).

May the road rise up to meet you,
May the wind be always at your back.
May the sun shine warm
Upon your face.

FROM THE GAELIC

MACGREGOR'S SCOTLAND

ALONG THE

Southern Upland Way

JIMMIE MACGREGOR

BBC BOOKS

By the same author

Jimmie Macgregor's Folk-Songs of Scotland (Jarrolds, Norwich).
Singing Our Own (Holmes McDougall).
On the West Highland Way (BBC Books).
Macgregor's Scotland: The Moray Coast, Speyside and the Cairngorms (BBC Books).
Macgregor's Scotland: In the Footsteps of Bonnie Prince Charlie (BBC Books).
Scottish Poetry from Macgregor's Gathering (BBC Books).
Macgregor's Gathering of Scottish Short Stories (BBC Books).
Macgregor's Gathering of Scottish Dialect Poetry (BBC Books).

Published by BBC Books,
a division of BBC Enterprises Limited,
Woodlands, 80 Wood Lane, London W12 0TT

First published 1990
© Jimmie Macgregor 1990

ISBN 0 563 20870 8

Set in 11 on 12pt Bembo by Ace Filmsetting Ltd, Frome, Somerset
Printed and bound in Great Britain by Richard Clay Ltd, Bungay
Cover printed by Richard Clay Ltd, Norwich

CONTENTS

ACKNOWLEDGEMENTS

WALKING AND filming on the Southern Upland Way was a wonderful experience for me, and I wish to thank the team who made the television series on which this book is mainly based: Dennis and Mary Dick of Wildview Productions (producer/director and production assistant, respectively), Brian Dewar who looked after the sound and Stanley Bradley who took the pictures. They provided a lot of laughs on the way, and cheerfully lugged equipment which the BBC describes as portable, and which probably is for about the first 100 metres of a 600-metre hill. What everyone else didn't carry, our sherpa, Spike Flack, did.

I'm also grateful to Walter Elliott, a poor but honest fencer, for his two poems, *The Twae Corbies* and *The Border Tongue*. Jim Mitchell of St Mary's Loch introduced me to *The Last Epistle to Tammas*, and Howard Purdie gave me *Tibbie Clovenfoot*.

Most importantly, I wish to thank all the people from coast to coast across the south of Scotland who generously gave of their knowledge, their stories, and their friendship.

PICTURE CREDITS

All photographs taken by Jimmie Macgregor.

INTRODUCTION

WHEN MY twenty-year singing partnership with Robin Hall came to an end, I found myself in the strange position of having time on my hands. My life as a folk musician, although exciting and enjoyable, had been a wildly hectic one, of concerts, clubs, theatres, radio, television, and travel travel travel. That was the easy part. It was the social life which was really demanding. The partnership had ended fairly abruptly, so that I was quite unprepared for the almost surreal experiences of going to bed before 2 a.m., seeing daylight in the mornings, and other bizarre phenomena of that nature. The adjustment was not easy – what was I to do with all these spare hours?

Gradually my son Gregor began to realise who I was, and I found myself enjoying this unaccustomed leisure. Not for long, however. Soon I was busying myself with my garden, ponds and aviaries, and I discovered that painting, pointing brickwork, and cleaning gutters was fun . . . for a while. There was the occasional concert – an odd experience after being half of a duet for so long – and I found that although I knew hundreds of harmony lines, I wasn't so hot on tunes. This was all very well, but by the time I had written a couple of folk song books to pass the time, I was getting restless. Consequently, when I read that the Countryside Commission for Scotland were planning a long-distance route, the West Highland Way, to run from just outside Glasgow to Fort William, I sat up and took notice. This was for me.

In my teens and student years I had tramped and camped in most of the areas to be traversed by the route, and I was much taken with the idea of renewing my acquaintance with these wonderful places. In the planning stages of my walk, I dashed off a note to the head of Radio Scotland, suggesting that there might be a programme to be made on the way.

After some discussion it was decided that we should go for six programmes. In the event, I took off with boots, rucksack and tape recorder, and returned with more than enough material for eight half-hour slots. The reaction to the programmes, rough as they were, was such that they were repeated on air four times, and I immediately followed up with a book for BBC Publications. The book, *On the West Highland Way*, became the basis for a BBC television series produced and directed by Dennis Dick of Wildview Productions.

The viewer response startled all concerned. The first transmission of the series was seen by more than 25 per cent of the Scottish population, and the networked repeats were equally well received. It was clear that we had struck a rich vein, and were providing something people really wanted.

I then presented a radio series and a television series on the Speyside Way and, in the following year, four television programmes in which I traced Prince Charles Edward Stuart's amazing escape route to France after the defeat at Culloden. This third series, entitled *In the Footsteps of Bonnie Prince Charlie*, took me to the outer isles, and led to yet another set of programmes, *On the Outer Edge*, which looked at life on some of the more remote Scottish islands.

The Southern Upland Way is the subject of the fifth television series, and the fourth book. In some ways, this has been the most interesting venture of all, if only because the south of Scotland is relatively unknown to the tourist or casual traveller. People from further south, especially, tend to see the west coast as the romantic target, and speed unheeding past one of the most beautiful and interesting areas of this most beautiful and interesting country.

My title *Along the Southern Upland Way* is chosen advisedly, for you will find in the book references to places and people not on the official route, but closely adjacent or related to the marked way. There is available an excellent set of two maps and two guide books covering the eastern and western sections of the route. These are published by Her Majesty's Stationery Office for the Countryside Commission for Scotland, and very well written by Ken Andrew. Everything the walker needs to know is to be found in these excellent publications.

My own book is a gathering of personal impressions in the course of two walks; the first for my ten-part radio series, and the second for Wildview Productions' six television programmes for the BBC, *Macgregor's Scotland*. General comments on equipment, the care of the countryside and such topics, are to be found in previous books in the *Macgregor's Scotland* series.

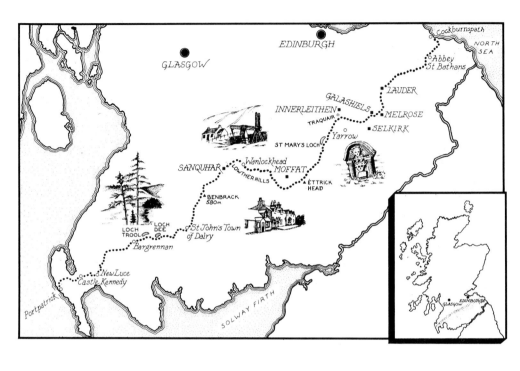

THE WAY

THE SOUTHERN Upland Way is the third of the Countryside Commission for Scotland's marked walkways, and at 340 kilometres is by far the longest – more than twice the length of the West Highland Way. Beginning at Portpatrick in the south-west of Scotland, the way crosses the whole width of Dumfries and Galloway, the southernmost part of Strathclyde, and traverses the superb border country all the way to the east coast, before doubling back a little way inland, to finish in the village of Cockburnspath, just south of Dunbar.

Phrases like 'the lush border country' and 'the rolling hills of the border' are quite descriptive, but can be misleading in some ways. The Southern Upland Way should certainly not be underestimated. It is a long, testing and even potentially hazardous trail, though with ordinary care the walker should suffer no more than the normal out-door hardships – soakings, sunburn, insect bites, sore muscles, and regrets about not staying at home before the television set.

Where most walks tend to follow the natural lines and contours of glens, old roads, paths and waterways, the Southern Upland Way is continually crossing these lines, and this undoubtedly adds to its rig-ours. The walk begins with coastal scenery and ends in the same way. In between, the walker follows old military roads, ancient tracks where the drovers herded their cattle and sheep, coach roads, farm tracks, and moorland and hill paths made by stalkers, shepherds, and by the sheep themselves. It can be claimed that of Scotland's three official marked walkways the Southern Upland Way offers the greatest variety, leading the walker through attractive towns and vil-lages, by picturesque loch sides and through great forests, across open grassland and moor, and up over the high hills. There are three main ranges in the Southern Uplands, the Galloway Hills, the Lowthers, and the Lammermuirs, and there will be times when the walker will be higher than at any point on the West Highland Way. The Lowthers rise to over 700 metres; Ben Brack is a punishing slog to 580 metres; and, in the James Hogg country, Ettrick Pen is 692 metres.

Lying directly on the route are Loch Trool and St Mary's Loch, the latter much used by enthusiastic sailors of small boats who enjoy the challenge of the sudden gusts which are funnelled down between the

1

hills. There are other extensive stretches of water, but these are man-made, though now well established and quite pleasing to the eye. Man-made features which may not be so pleasing to many people are the wide areas of commercial forest in southern Scotland. In some places there is mile after mile of dark green sitka spruce stretching as far as the eye can see, and walking through the dark tunnels of the forest paths can sometimes be tedious and uninteresting.

There is, however, compensation to be found in the great variety of wildlife. The endless range of differing habitats on the Southern Upland Way means that there is a chance of seeing almost anything at some point during your journey. There are exotic creatures like wild goats, ring ouzels and merlins, and on several occasions I had good sightings of hen harriers, short-eared owls, and peregrine falcons. Kestrels and buzzards are commonplace; the calls of the moorland birds enhance the charm of the high, lonely places, and there is enough mixed woodland on the lower ground to support the sparrowhawk and the small birds on which it depends. The mature coniferous forests have crossbills, capercaillie, coal-tits, siskins and goldcrests, while most of the common birds nest around the lighter fringes of the woods. The proliferation of forest has greatly increased the numbers of the little roe deer, and if you move reasonably quietly, you will certainly see them. The red deer are much easier, for there is a herd of them in the Galloway Forest Park.

The character of the whole of the Southern Uplands has been fashioned by its history. In earlier times, the border between England and Scotland shifted and changed with the fortunes of war, and until the union of the crowns in 1603, power was in the hands of powerful feuding families. Cattle reiving was practised as a matter of course, and people of wealth and influence protected themselves in fortified houses whose ruins still remind us of those turbulent times. However, when King James VI of Scotland became James I of England, the power of the great families was curtailed in an effort to bring law and stability to the area. The bearing of arms was proscribed and the defence works of the fortified houses were removed. The jolly days of the cattle reivers were over. They mended their ways, they fled, or they were strung up, and within a relatively short period life in the south of Scotland became settled enough for proper agriculture to develop.

To the west, Galloway was less affected by this warring way of life, but suffered greatly during the 'Killing Times' when the Covenanters who resisted the imposition of a new form of worship were fiercely persecuted. There are many reminders of these terrible times along the way, as there are of the great religious centres such as Melrose Abbey. Great estates were established, splendid parks and gardens laid out, and grand houses built. There are probably more stately homes and castles in the south of Scotland than in any other area. Many lie on, or adjacent to, the walkers' route: the ruined Castle Kennedy, Lochinch Castle, Abbotsford, Thirlestane, Traquair and Drumlanrig, among others.

Anyone interested in poetry and balladry will know that the Scottish border country has produced a wealth of material, from the traditional songs, legends and ballads so beloved by Hogg and Burns to the more sophisticated romantic works of Sir Walter Scott. The south of Scotland still has its songsmiths and story-tellers. If you're as lucky as I have been, perhaps you will meet some of them on your journey along the Southern Upland Way.

PORTPATRICK: SMUGGLERS AND A CARELESS NANNY

A GLANCE AT a map of the south of Scotland will show that Portpatrick lies on the outer edge of a strangely shaped promontory which is almost cut off from the mainland by Loch Ryan to the north and Luce Bay to the south. This area is known as the Rhins of Galloway, and the first section of the Southern Upland Way crosses it from Portpatrick to a point above Loch Ryan.

Portpatrick is named for the patron saint of Ireland, which lies a mere 35 kilometres across the North Channel. In the clear, sharp, sunny weather which I encountered on my first visit, it seemed almost within shouting distance, with the chimney of the power station near Carrickfergus clearly visible.

Colourfully painted and beautifully clean, Portpatrick is built around a horseshoe-shaped bay, and used to be a very important place indeed. At one time, it was the chief departure point for Ireland, and countless craft of all kinds have plied back and forth for centuries. In the late eighteenth century a proper harbour was built, but although it was later improved upon by the great Thomas

Telford, it was never really successful. Gradually Portpatrick was supplanted by bigger ports, especially the one at Stranraer.

I was intrigued by the buildings of the Portpatrick radio station, which stands at the high point of the cliff-top path, so, in my quest for information, I applied a technique highly developed, honed, and fine tuned over the years. I banged on the door and asked. The manager of the station, Geoff Brown, showed me round and introduced me to his operators Robert Hare and Graham Mercer, weather-man Mike Scarrat and handyman Sandy Gibson. Geoff told me that the Post Office took over the station in the 1920s, and that it is used by British Telecom and the coastguard to maintain contact with ships in the area. This can involve anything from accidents at sea, rescue operations or news of someone's wife giving birth. Nothing, however, as dramatic as a message I once overheard on a policeman's radio in a theatre bar. 'Tango Orange Zeppelin [*or something like that*] calling. Mayday! Mayday! Bring chips. Bring chips.'

Leaving the radio station, I found that the dark grey sandstone cliffs and gullies had given way to steep, grassy slopes to the sea, with Dunskey golf course on the right. Dunskey House and estate lie a little inland, and Ross Cunningham, whom I met on my first visit, told me something about them. Ross is very interested in the area, though he is not really a local. His family came from Newton Stewart, about 30 kilometres away; but that was only thirty years ago, and proper qualification as a local takes more like 300 years.

Dunskey House is built of stone from the much more ancient Dunskey Castle, which, with its twin on the Irish coast, kept an eye on shipping in the North Channel, and levied toll on the old 'pay up

Portpatrick: the
lifeboat

Near Dunskey Glen

or else' principle. It was Ross Cunningham who told me the story of
the maid who was left in charge of the baby, and rather carelessly
dropped it from a high window into the sea. Having given careful
thought to the probable consequences, she threw herself over too.

Another man with an encyclopaedic knowledge of the area's history is Alfred Truckle, whom I interviewed on my radio programme
some time before I undertook the walk. Alf told me that over a very
long period the whole area was involved in smuggling; in fact it only
began to die down after 1800. Its heyday was in the early 1700s, and
the main trade was with the Isle of Man. Salt was heavily taxed at that
time, so that it became even more important than silks and brandies.

The smugglers were a daring, hard-nosed lot, prepared to risk life
and limb, especially other people's, for the rich pickings of their
trade. However, many ordinary people were involved in buying,
trading, protecting the smugglers, and waging continuous guerrilla
war on the excisemen.

The most famous of these excisemen was Robert Burns, who lived
near here for a time. It seems a bizarre profession for a man of his
known radical and anti-establishment views, but by all accounts he
was rather good at it. The first official report on him says, 'Robert
Burns the poet does well,' and at the time of his death he had been
scheduled for promotion to supervisor at Leith. His humanity was
brought to bear even on this job, however, and although he did his
duty in bearing down heavily on the real law-breakers, he is known
to have passed a word of warning to the occasional old wifie doing a
little brewing on the side.

WRONG TURNINGS AND
ROLLING SHEEP

WHERE DUNSKEY Glen meets the shoreline, a little bridge leads over to a stony beach, at the far end of which the walker is confronted by a rather formidable-looking cliff. It's puzzling that the path appears to head directly towards it, but on closer inspection you find that it creeps behind a huge slice of the cliff which has become detached from the face. It then follows some stumbling ups and downs, and twists and turns, before arriving at the ascent.

This turns out to be less daunting than it looks from the far end of the beach. The cliff is not really all that high, and is broken up by a series of rough, rocky steps and footholds. The climb is made easier by a chain set into stanchions in the rock, and a little hauling and huffing and puffing takes you up on to open, grassy land leading to the Killantringan lighthouse.

The light was established here in 1900, replacing one at Portpatrick, and has the distinction of having had a shipwreck on its doorstep. In 1982 the coaster *Craigantlet*, en route for Liverpool, sailed straight across the Channel, and, embarrassingly, ran on to the rocks a few yards away from the lighthouse. There must have been much jocular speculation at the time as to how such a spectacular misjudgement could have been made. However, Irish readers may console themselves with the knowledge that the ship was Cypriot registered. Not so funny was the fact that the ship was carrying toxic waste, which leaked into the sea as she broke up, causing serious pollution. The lighthouse was evacuated, and the public were barred from the area. After some time, 'official assurances' were given that the place was now safe, but you are still requested to remain outside the fence, which has been erected to assure you of how safe it is.

Turning inland shortly after leaving Killantringan, I encountered what was to be the first of many cattle grids on the route. The cattle grid is a brilliantly simple device for preventing animals from straying. It consists simply of a concreted pit across a road or track, roofed with spaced iron rails or flattened bars. Animals won't cross them, but they present no problems to wheels. Walkers wishing to avoid sprained ankles should negotiate them with care. Hedgehogs should avoid them altogether, but they don't – often falling between the

The Killantringan lighthouse

rails, becoming trapped in the pit, and starving to death. Little ramps are now being built in to provide escape routes for dopy hedgehogs, and I've been told that in some parts of Wales, sheep have learned to lie down and *roll* over the grids. I'd love to believe that.

A few miles of pleasant, gradually rising farmland takes you to the cairn on Mulloch Hill, the highest point on the walk so far. On both my visits here, I was fortunate in encountering clear, sunny, breezy weather on this wonderful open hill pasture. The meadow flowers bloomed in profusion, skylarks exulted overhead, and the views were exhilarating, with Loch Ryan gleaming below. At Cairnryan, on my first trip, the ship breakers were reducing to scrap an aircraft carrier which had done service in the Falklands – a sad, and rather ugly sight among all this beauty. Sunlight gleamed on the water, and beyond the bulk of Ailsa Craig, the ragged outline of Arran was clearly visible, bringing back happy memories of tramping and camping on that lovely island. From here, the way leads above and past Loch Ryan, to descend to the village of Castle Kennedy through some fine mixed woodland.

CASTLE KENNEDY: BOOLERS
AND A BLUFF COVE

Twixt Wigton and the town of Air;
Portpatrick and the cruives* of Cree†,
No man needs think for to bide there,
Unless he court with Kennedie.

T HE KENNEDYS were a tough and powerful lot, and held sway here from about the middle of the fifteenth century. Castle Kennedy was built in 1607, and was accidentally razed by fire in 1716. The Kennedys, though very successful indeed for a time, did not, perhaps, have as keen an eye for the buttered side of the bread as their Campbell counterparts in the west Highlands, and ultimately their support for the Covenanters brought them down. The estates were acquired by Sir James Dalrymple, who became Viscount Stair in 1690. Dalrymple was a very able man: professor at Glasgow University, lawyer, soldier and statesman. Although strictly speaking on the other side, he resisted the excesses against the Covenanters, at great risk to his own career, and at one point had to flee the country.

His son became the first Earl of Stair, but is remembered in Scotland with rather less affection. The union with England in 1707 was organised by a group with Stair at its head, the hated 'Parcel of Rogues' described by Robert Burns in his ferocious song. For most Scots, the part Stair played in the infamous massacre of Glencoe in 1692 left an even blacker stain on his character. Stair hated all Jacobites, clan McDonald in particular, and enthusiastically carried out an instruction from King William to 'Extirpate this sept of theives'. The circumstances were dubious, the method of execution was reprehensible, and there was an outcry. Stair was accused of 'over-zealousness and barbarity', but predictably he was exonerated, and given a pension for his troubles.

The present Earl of Stair is what often used to be described in a certain type of novel as a 'bluff old cove', and is often to be seen wandering around his beloved grounds dressed in corduroy trousers and an old tweed jacket. Visitors are sometimes a little wary of this rather large man wielding a billhook, but the Earl explained to me

---

* *cruives* = curves   † *Cree* = the River Cree

8

The Earl of Stair and family

that he wages constant war on weeds, and always has the billhook at hand. I found him a charming and amusing man. He took great pleasure in demonstrating the little golf buggy in which he goes buzzing around the estate, and pointed out its two holders for Martini glasses. 'Very American, that,' he observed. He and his wife and son made me most welcome, and seemed devoid of the silly snobbery which seems to afflict people a few notches further down the accepted social scale.

The Earl of Stair is rightly proud of his grounds, for they are truly magnificent, and in the spring and early summer the variety and richness of magnolias, rhododendrons and azaleas is overwhelming. The second Earl of Stair, son of John Dalrymple, was responsible for laying out the grounds. He was at one time ambassador to France and had been much impressed by the Palace of Versailles. The work at Castle Kennedy was made less tiresome, and certainly less expensive, by using the men and equipment of the Royal Scots Greys and the Inniskilling Fusiliers – a bit cheeky really, and not something which would be readily countenanced today.

The present home of the Earl and Countess is Lochinch Castle, which was built in 1867. There are two lochs on the estate, the Black Loch and the White Loch, joined by a canal. The island on the Black Loch is a crannog, an ancient man-made island, and has a well-

Castle Kennedy 'boolers'

established heronry, while on a smaller island there is a raucous colony of black-headed gulls.

Having met Jackie Johnston who runs the tea-room, and John McArthur Moir, the head gardener, I had one final call to make before leaving Castle Kennedy. This was to the bowling club, whose beautifully situated greens and clubhouse were built for the estate workers. The club's president, Eric McQuistin, introduced me to the club members, a friendly lot, and after endless tea and buns, I was fortified enough for the next stage of my journey.

LEPERS, LUNKIES AND BELTIES

THERE IS a beautiful view back to Castle Kennedy from the track which rises steadily above Chlenry farm. This is a very pleasant walk on a good path lined with hawthorn, and rich with the colours of wayside flowers, and it was here that I had the good fortune to meet Willie Hardie, who has been a keeper on the Stair estate all of his working life. The Stairs were good employers, he told me, but he'd seen the whole style of estate management changing. My impression was that he didn't see much change for the better. Where there might have been twelve or fifteen keepers on an estate, there would now be one, with an estate manager.

I remarked on the fact that Willie's dogs Dinah and Josie were black labradors, and was told that this was a tradition on the estate. He was well satisfied with the breed, and obviously took their training very seriously. He preferred bitches to dogs, finding them sharper, but easier to control. There were obviously problems when they came into season, but that could be overcome by injections, or by sprayed powders which killed their alluring odour. But the best solution, Willie felt, was to leave bitches in season at home. On one occasion, one of his favourites, having been sent into the water to retrieve a duck, was hotly pursued by an amorous and powerful dog. Having achieved his objective, he vigorously set about the business in hand, ungallantly ignoring the fact that the object of his passion

Above Chlenry

Willie Hardie

11

Glen Luce Abbey

was totally submerged. Only Willie's prompt rescue action saved the poor bitch from a fate worse than the one which is supposed to be worse than death.

The path above Chlenry opens out on to an upland walk which is a delight in fine weather, but the forest track to New Luce was closed for bridge building when I came that way, and I was forced on to the diversion by the road. I wasn't too pleased about this, and shared a moan with the first real way walkers I had encountered so far, Ken Watson of Falkirk and Alastair Pettigrew from Stirling. These lads were travelling light, had a daily schedule carefully worked out, with accommodation pre-booked, and generally seemed to know what they were about.

New Luce is an attractive, well-kept wee place, boasting a church, a shop, and a pub. Its main claim to fame is that the Covenanter Alexander Peden preached here. Like others of his kind, Peden the Prophet, as he was called, was continuously harried and persecuted for his beliefs, but unlike many, he survived to die a natural death. I was lucky enough to meet the oldest inhabitant of New Luce, John McGuire, a good-natured man who had a lot to say about changes in the village. As in so many parts of Scotland, these changes were mainly due to the influx from the south.

Not far from the village is the stabilised ruin of Glen Luce Abbey. This ancient Cistercian abbey is well worth the diversion, and is cared for by the Department of the Environment. It's said that lepers came here to be blessed, on their way to the leper colony at Liberland.

On the way to Bargrennan, I renewed my acquaintance with John McIlwrick who farms at Balmurrie. John is a tenant of the Earl of Stair and has been at Balmurrie for forty years. He and his wife invited me in for tea and cake, and I asked them if they ever had trouble with the way walkers. The way passes between John's farm steadings, but he had no complaints, except about dogs. 'Even quite reasonable people seem to be unreasonable about their dogs,' he said. I assured him that in the town, too, people were becoming more and more concerned about the nuisance and danger levels. I was amused to hear John complaining about the fine weather I had been enjoying, and he quoted the old rhyme,

Rain in May brings the hay.

Near John McIlwrick's farm, I came across my first lunky. Also known as a smout, this is simply a hole in a dry stane dyke. It's just big enough for sheep to pass through one at a time, but it bars cattle. The gap can be easily closed, and it's a simple and effective way of controlling stock.

The way from here to Bargrennan involves both woodland and moorland walking, and the two main points of interest are the standing stones at Laggangarn, and the nearby Wells of the Rees. The stones are large, impressive slabs, dating from the eighth century. Each of the two monuments bears a large cross with four smaller ones incised into the angles. The ancient Wells of the Rees, which lie slightly off the way, consist of three little springs roofed over with stones, and it is said that the lepers used to refresh themselves here.

Further on, at Derry farm, I came upon my first belted Galloway

A 'lunky'

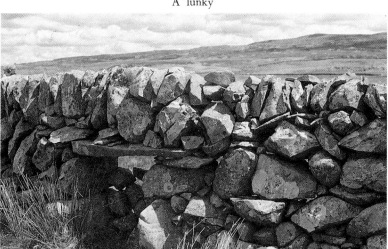

cattle. These impressive beasts are very distinctive indeed – jet black animals with a wide band of white encircling the body. The herd here is owned by Miss Flora Stuart of the Mochrum estate. Miss Stuart is president of the Belted Galloway Society, but it was stockman Alex McKnight who told me about them.

Alex is wildly enthusiastic about the breed, finding them hardy, easily managed and productive. Some people cross the belties with the continental giants, the Charollais and Simmentals, resulting in huge calves which can damage or even kill the mothers in labour.

Alex shared the general horror in the area that the much-loved belties were to be replaced as the symbol of Dumfries and Galloway by a goose, or as one outraged worthy put it to me, 'a blank-blank duck'.

The Gallowa' Hills

For I'll tak my plaidie* contented tae be,
A wee bittie kilted abune† my knee;
I'll gie my pipes anither blaw,
And I'll gang oot ower the hills tae Gallowa'.

Oh the Gallowa' hills are covered wi' broom,
Wi' heather bells and bonnie bloom;
Wi' heather bells and rivers a',
And I'll gang oot ower‡ the hills tae Gallowa'.

For I said, 'Bonnie lassie, will ye come wi' me,
Tae share my lot in a strange countrie;
Tae share my lot, when doon fa's a',§
And I'll gang oot ower the hills tae Gallowa'.'

Oh the Gallowa' hills, etc.

For I'll sell my rock, I'll sell my reel,
I'll sell my Granny's spinning wheel;
I'll sell the lot when doon fa's a',
And I'll gang oot ower the hills tae Gallowa'.

Oh the Gallowa' hills, etc.

---

* *plaidie* = plaid † *abune* = above ‡ *gang oot ower* = go out over
§ *doon fa's a'* = down falls all (loosely, when times are hard)

This song started life as *The Braes of Galloway*, and is attributed to William Nicolson, an old ballad singer who died about the middle of the nineteenth century, but these are the words given to me by the great traditional singer, Jeannie Robertson. Jeannie sang the song in grand, measured ballad style, but Robin Hall and I recorded it in a kind of swaggering march tempo, and that's the way it has been done ever since.

MARTYRS AND MONUMENTS

ON THE way to Bargrennan, Ochiltree Hill, though only about 180 metres in height, commands fine, extensive views, and offers a useful general impression of the surrounding countryside. This wide open area would once have been covered in forest, and the thick growth on the islands in the loch demonstrates the contrast between ground which has been grazed by deer and sheep, and that which has been left to normal regeneration. But the natural forests of old are now being replaced by vast, dark areas of commercial forestry. From the Ochiltree viewpoint, a striking example of this is seen in the Galloway Forest Park. Also visible from here is Glen Trool, and at some distance the Merrick, the highest hill in the Southern Uplands at over 840 metres. In fine weather, many other points can be identified with the aid of a map.

The Martyrs' Monument on Wigton's Windy Hill is clearly seen from the high point of Ochiltree. The obelisk honours all the Covenanting martyrs who died in the Killing Times. All along the way we see more and more evidence of the impact of this period on the south of Scotland. I have already noted Peden the Prophet's connection with New Luce. In the same area as the Wells of the Rees and the standing stones at Laggangarn is the tomb of Alex Linn. Linn was an ordinary shepherd and a devout man, who was killed in 1685 by Lieutenant-General Drummond. The Windy Hill monument reminds us of sixty-three-year-old Margaret McLaughlan and eighteen-year-old Margaret Wilson who died for their faith. They were tied to wooden stakes and left to drown in the incoming tide at the mouth of the River Bladnoch at Wigton. Stone markers and monuments to the martyrs of the Covenant are to be found in cemeteries, on hillsides and out-of-the-way places all along the route.

THE ROE AND THE RED; FOREST
AND FRUIT CAKE

IN THE Glen Trool forest I met Willie Laurie, who used to farm this area before it was planted. The forest here is quite mixed, and much lighter and more spacious than the dense single-species plantations, but Willie says that he isn't so aware of the hills now as he goes about his business. Willie Laurie is a big, friendly man, of a type I've often met in the country, and he obviously loves his surroundings. He talked at some length about the changes wrought by the forest. There were more bird species, he believed, though the birds of the open hill – curlew, peewit, wheatear, pipit and the like – had gone. Willie runs a few sheep and cows, but is now employed by the Forestry Commission as a wildlife ranger, concerned mainly with deer.

The roe deer, once a fairly rare animal, has built up its numbers dramatically with the increase in forestry. It can do much damage, so has to be carefully controlled. In this fairly open type of woodland, the red deer has become once again a forest animal, and with good shelter and food, and a generally easier life than on the open hill, has become much larger and heavier. The Glen Trool forest red deer are quite unusual, though not unique, but basically the habits and habitat of the red and the roe are quite different, as are the animals themselves.

A red deer stag will stand about 1.2 metres at the shoulder, and with a good head will tower away over 1.8 metres and can weigh 130 kg. The roe buck is about 76 centimetres at the shoulder. The females of the two species are known as hinds and does respectively,

Glen Trool
forest

Willie Laurie

and the young are calves and kids. Where the red stag has the dramatic branching spread of antler presented to the world by Edwin Landseer in his famous painting *The Monarch of the Glen*, the roe buck has small, but rather dangerous prongs.

The roe deer rut and mating take place in July and August, and this is when they break with their normal silent and secret habits, uttering loud barking challenges to rivals, and generally becoming much bolder and more aggressive in their behaviour. The red deer mate much later in the autumn, and the hoarse roaring, or 'belling', of the rutting stags is one of the most exciting sounds of the high hills. The roe is usually seen singly or in small family groups, whilst, except at mating time, the red deer run in sometimes quite large herds, the stags and hinds in separate groups.

Roe deer have developed an interesting breeding technique known as delayed implantation. They mate at a time of year when food is plentiful and they are likely to be in good physical condition, but the development of the embryo does not begin until the time is right for the young to be born into good conditions. Roe deer normally have twins and sometimes triplets, while the red deer on the hill will have a single calf. If you find a young deer, don't be tempted to remove, or even touch it. The foraging mother knows exactly where it is, and the human scent may force her to abandon her offspring to starvation or predators.

Willie Laurie obviously takes a great interest in the creatures in his charge, and loves the place where he lives. He enjoys seeing the otters in the early mornings, and close by his house a redstart was brooding her clutch of blue eggs, a few feet from a pied flycatcher nesting in the same tree. I had a break for tea and a chat with the

Lauries, and I can tell you, hand on heart, that Willie's daughter Margaret makes the best fruit cake in the known universe.

OLD MORTALITY, CANNIBALISM
AND NEW GAMES

A T CALDONS Wood there is a fairly elaborate martyrs' tomb, in memory of six Covenanters who were caught here in the act of worship, and summarily shot by Colonel Douglas, Lieutenant Livingston and Cornet James Douglas. The inscription tells us that they were 'Most impiously and cruelly murthered for their adherence to Scotland's Reformation Covenants, and Solemn League, 1685'. A stonemason called Robert Paterson made it his life's work to travel around restoring and maintaining these Covenanting monuments, and he became the model for Sir Walter Scott's *Old Mortality*. Scott describes him in this way:

> *An old man was seated upon the monument of the slaughtered presbyterians, and busily employed in deepening, with his chisel, the letters of the inscription, which, announcing, in scriptural language, the promised blessings of futurity to be the lot of the slain, anathematised the murderers with corresponding violence. A blue bonnet of unusual dimensions covered the grey hairs of the pious workman. His dress was a large old-fashioned coat of the coarse cloth called hodden grey, usually worn by the elder peasants, with waistcoat and breeches of the same: and the whole suit, though still in decent repair, had obviously seen a train of long service.*

Paterson's loving care was undone in more recent times by vandals who smashed the stone. It was pieced together and is now safe in the Newton Stewart museum – the one in Caldons Wood is a replica.

The camping and caravan site at Caldons Wood is a far cry from those dreadful geometrical van villages which can ruin a beautiful place. The area is open and grassy with a random scattering of fine old mature trees, and the vans and tents are distributed in a pleasantly random manner. Jim Hamilton, the forestry manager, showed me around and pointed out features like the shop and drying facilities. As Jim guided me along the path by the shore of Loch Trool, he told me a story which was a mixture of the comic and the horrific. A colleague who conducted young people on a nature trail was delighted to find a nest of blue tits only a few metres away from the nest of a woodpecker. He took great pleasure in taking some young people to see the arrangement, but was slightly embarrassed to discover that the woodpecker too had located the blue tit's nest and was happily feeding blue tit chicks to the young woodpeckers.

Above Loch Trool, there is a gigantic boulder known as the Bruce's Stone, which commemorates one of King Robert the Bruce's victories over the English. The forest track by Loch Trool was found to be tortuous and muddy, and was re-routed closer to the loch shore, despite some opposition from the people who own Glen Trool Lodge and the loch itself, the Moores, of Littlewood's Pools.

One of the less pleasant aspects of the Southern Upland Way is that the area is very much used by screaming, low-flying jet planes playing war games. 'Wee boys wi' big toys', as one disgruntled farmer put it. What is worse is that one crashes every now and then, costing lives, and millions of pounds of taxpayers' money.

DEATH IN THE HILLS

THE DUMFRIES and Galloway area is well used to plane crashes, as I learned some years ago when I interviewed a man called Tommy Withers, from Hurlford, Kilmarnock. Tommy is a keen hill walker, and by a happy coincidence I met him on a hill above Loch Dee, during my Southern Upland Way walk.

Loch Trool

Loch Dee

He told me that close on 500 planes had come to grief in Dumfries and Galloway. During the last war, there were numerous training fields in the south of Scotland, at Wigton, West Freugh, Castle Kennedy, Heathall, and other places. A tremendous amount of air traffic was generated, and there was much night flying. Tommy Withers pointed out that most of the casualties were caused not by enemy action, but by young and inexperienced pilots refusing to believe their instruments, coming down to look for landmarks, and being confronted by the face of a hill. Many of the aircraft were underpowered and could not lift out of trouble quickly enough.

Cairnsmore of Fleet, which rises to 710 metres, has so far claimed five Ansons, two Bothas, an American Phantom, and a German Heinkel which was bound for Belfast with a load of land mines. When it exploded, the crewmen were blown to bits, and the tail section of the aircraft landed over three-quarters of a kilometre away. In 1940 a Whitley bomber crashed at the foot of the Merrick and careered into Loch Enoch. The plane was missing for eleven days until reported by a shepherd lad. The bodies of two crewmen were recovered; the third lies with the plane in the depths of the loch, and the crash site has been declared a War Grave.

20

A Dornier bomber, intent on slaughter over Clydebank, was chased off by Spitfires and shot down at Monquhill Farm, by Carsphairn. One can still see the gap in the dry stane dyke where the Dornier's tail wheel struck it. The pilot bravely stayed with the aircraft and was killed, while his crew, who had baled out, spent the night in a sheep stell* before being arrested by the local police. The pilot is buried at Traquair. A young lad took a machine gun from the crash site, but found that he couldn't get it home on his bicycle. It was buried by the roadside, and has never been recovered.

THIRTY-NINE STEPS AND MORE

ETWEEN LOCH Trool and Loch Dee is the wide open country chosen by John Buchan for the famous chase in his novel *The Thirty-Nine Steps*. If you haven't read the book, you may have seen the television series in which the elegant figure of actor Robert Powell puffed and stumbled over what was supposed to be this stretch of upland. Buchan gives a graphic description of the terrain.

> *I sat down on the very crest of the pass and took stock of my position. In front was a flat space of maybe a mile, all pitted with bog holes and rough with tussocks; and then, beyond it, the road fell steeply down another glen whose blue dimness melted into the distance. To left and right were round-shouldered green hills as smooth as pancakes, but to the south, that is, the left hand, there was a glimpse of high heathery mountains which I remembered from the map as the big knot of hill which I had chosen for my sanctuary. I was on the central boss of a huge upland country, and could see everything for miles.*

Coming down from this huge boss of country, I made my way to the White Laggan Bothy and Loch Dee, where I had arranged to meet Ian Murray, who is the fish ranger responsible for the loch. Ian told me something of the problems of stocking the loch, and especially the acid rain menace. The efforts of Ian and his colleagues appear to be successful, as the loch is very popular, and I met fishers who had been coming back here year after year.

---

* *stell* = pen or fold

Wild billy goat

Jack Rutherford

After much study, it has been discovered that the older fish can become resistant to the acid rain and other pollutants, but that the eggs, alevins and fry are very vulnerable indeed. In the streams where they hatch, they are attacked not only by the acid rain, but also by the acidity caused by forestry. The loch is stocked with brown trout and the technique is to rear them away from the streams, and introduce them to the loch at a later stage.

Monitoring is also carried out at three separate streams: the trees around the first have been clear felled; around the second they are allowed to grow fairly close; and the third has trees to the water's edge. It is hoped that this will give a more precise picture of the effects of forestry on the lochs and the fish.

At Clatteringshaws Loch, the deer museum is well worth a visit, and nearby is yet another stone commemorating a victory by Robert the Bruce, this one in 1307. In the tourist season, it is usually quite easy to see the wild goats which live in the area. They are truly wild in the sense that they are in no way farmed or tended, but they are not so wild in that they have learned that there are easy pickings from tourists, and they can be enticed to the roadside fence, where they enjoy a diet of crisps, Mars bars and cucumber sandwiches.

Between Craigenbay and Glen Garroch, I came upon a surprisingly good track through very rough ground, and I discovered, working beside it, someone whom I knew. He is countryside ranger Richard Mearns, and he looked rather different in this setting – wielding a spade, wellies deep in soggy peat, and hair plastered to his face by an insistent drizzle. Richard has done extensive research over a number of years on the peregrine falcons of the south of Scotland,

and some time ago I interviewed his wife Barbara about a book which they had written together.

The book is entitled *Biographies of Birdwatchers*, and it mentions three famous Scots. In Millport Bay, Dr Peter McDougall first identified the beautiful roseate tern which now bears his name, *Stena dougalli*. Francis Buchanan Hamilton, who was born in Callander, gave his name to the grey-necked bunting, *Emberiza buchani*. Probably the most famous of all Scottish ornithologists is Alexander Wilson, of Wilson's phalarope and Wilson's petrel. Wilson was a Paisley weaver who was jailed for his radical views, and on his release went to America. He was astounded and fascinated by the variety and richness of the bird life of the New World, produced a huge volume of wonderful drawings and paintings, and to this day is known as the father of American ornithology.

WATER POWER AND A
FUNNY FAMILY

COMING DOWN through Glen Garroch, I reached the Earlstoun power station where I was met by Jack Rutherford, who had shown me round on my last visit. Jack, who was at the point of retirement when I last saw him, was station attendant at Kendoon, and when I commented that the stations reminded me of the engine-rooms of the big ships, he told me that the lads in the station take a great pride in the installations. This was evident in the impeccable paintwork and glowing brass and copper. In the

Galloway Hydro Electric Scheme, the other stations are Kendoon, Carsfad, Glenlee, and the largest, Tongland, which is at Kirkcudbright. There are eight dams, and as Jack explained, the principle is quite simple.

The dams store the water, which is guided through pipes four metres in diameter. These lead to the great turbines, and the sheer pressure of the water on the blades creates the power which generates the electricity. The beauty of the system lies in its simplicity. Water is free (at the time of writing) and we have plenty of it in Scotland. Maintenance is minimal, and these installations have been giving steady service since the 1930s. At Earlstoun, 7112 kilograms of water per second turns the turbines at 214 revolutions per minute to produce 14 000 kilowatts from two turbines – a modest output compared to a place like Longannet, which can produce 2 400 000 kilowatts.

Dam attendant and weatherman Stuart McSkimming took me to the summit of Glenlee Hill, and explained that 152 metres below us was a tunnel carrying water underground for 5.6 kilometres from the man-made Clatteringshaws Loch to Kendoon. This was just one mind-boggling achievement in a superb civil engineering project conceived and initiated in the middle of the great economic depression of the Thirties (Earlstoun power station was completed in 1936). The whole concept was the brainchild of two local men, Major Wellwood Maxwell and Captain Scott Elliott, and with civil engineer Colonel William McClelland they made their dream reality. What amazes and pleases me, as someone interested in design and conservation, is that the power stations represent the best in functional, clean-lined Thirties architecture, and the dams are beauti-

Stuart
McSkimming

The fish ladder
at Earlstoun

fully sculpted into their surroundings. One type of dam has its strength in sheer bulk, and others, called arch and gravity dams, are curved to resist the colossal pressure of the water. Excess water is drained off by spill gates, or floodgates, which, when fully opened, present a spectacle to remember.

These designers and builders were conservationists long before the word became a slogan. The stations are well landscaped and planted, and sometimes even include fish ladders leading back up to the traditional spawning grounds. At the big station at Tongland, the fish are counted electronically and, in a good season, thousands leap the ladder at Earlstoun. The chaos and the racket, the ring of the hammers and the shouts of the workmen have long since vanished into silence, leaving us monumental, handsome, man-made structures which complement the landscape in which they exist. I am grateful to Phil Gallie, station manager of the Galloway Hydro Electric Scheme, and to Jack Rutherford and his colleagues John McGowran and Rob Douglas for explaining the workings of the scheme, and for making me so welcome.

Before we parted company, Jack Rutherford took me to one of the dams where, he assured me, there was a barn owl's nest which was rather unusual. When we arrived, I discovered that it was possible to look down a shaft which gave a clear view without disturbing the bird. By sheer good fortune, the owl was off the eggs, and I could see what had so interested Jack. The barn owl had obviously ousted a nesting kestrel from what was rather a good site, but not before the kestrel had laid her full complement of five rust-coloured eggs. The owl had then added her own clutch of white, almost perfectly round eggs, making a total of nine.

It was interesting to speculate what would have happened had all the eggs hatched. Kestrels and owls eat much the same things. When young they both look like a ball of cotton wool with a beak, and assuming that there was an adequate food supply in the area, and that two owls on overdrive were capable of feeding such a freakish family, there was no real reason that it shouldn't have worked. Sadly, the kestrel's eggs had obviously chilled, but the barn owls successfully reared their brood.

When I went back in another season to film in the area it was the owls who had been ousted, and five fat, smug-looking kestrel chicks were very much in possession.

DALRY: JOHN THE BAPTIST AND ROBBIE THE SHEPHERD

FILMING FOR the Southern Upland Way television series took me to the delightful village of St Johns Town of Dalry for the third time. My first visit was in the course of my radio series, and on the second occasion I stayed in the village for several days while making a video about the hydro-electric schemes in the area. (The video is shown on a regular basis to the tourists at the Tongland visitors' centre.) So lots of people know me in the village, and this created some problems for producer/director Dennis Dick, and for Stan Bradley and Brian Dewar on camera and sound, for each time we began to film, people would call or wave, open doors and windows to shout greetings, or stop me to talk. All very friendly and pleasant, but it held up the action a bit. However, the folk in Dalry soon caught on, and in no time were behaving like seasoned actors.

Dalry is an attractive, beautifully kept little place. The houses sparkle with new paint, and the gardens are superb. It is a model village and they have awards to prove it. It is difficult to believe that in Covenanting times Dalry was seething with unrest and bitterness against the government. This ended in a march to Edinburgh, which had bloody consequences for the Covenanters. The cemetery has more of the Covenanters' graves which are a recurring feature along the route. There's no doubt that the religious fanaticism was on both sides, though the Covenanters were certainly the victims of savage persecution. However, it was a presbyterian kirk session at Dalry in

St John's Town of Dalry

1698 which condemned Elspeth McEwan as a witch, and it was pres-byterians who roasted her alive at Kirkcudbright.

The main street of Dalry is on quite a steep slope, and from the fountain at the bottom of the village, every house is painted a different colour, and bedecked with flowers, all the way to where the road forks at the top of the hill. At this point, there is an indented stone which is remarkably comfortable to sit on, and is known as John the Baptist's seat, for reasons which remain obscure. Even the most romantic resident would find it difficult to believe that John the Baptist would have had any pressing reason to visit Dalry. The name St John's Town of Dalry is said to have been given by the Knights Templar, who were organised to protect pilgrims en route to the Holy Land.

In the village street I met Mr and Mrs Hurst, who run a Southern Upland Way support vehicle, picking up and dropping off walkers who are tackling the way in sections. I was also delighted to avail myself of the hospitality of Dr and Mrs Rhymer, whose house looks on to John the Baptist's seat. The Rhymers are a very likeable couple from the south who, having been visitors for twenty years, have now settled in the village so that Dr Rhymer can pursue his writing. They are well integrated and are now considered locals. Dalry, like almost every place along the way, has a quite astonishing percentage of incomers, and there is no doubt that the whole character of the place is changing very rapidly.

On leaving Dalry, I was taken to see retired shepherd Robbie Murray. I was met at the cottage door by a rugged-looking man, obviously diminished by age, but still an imposing figure. As greetings were exchanged, he produced a bottle, two glasses and a fiddle, in a gesture of hospitality which had clearly become ritualised over many years. Music was very important to Robbie, growing up as he did at a time when country folk made their own entertainment. His father and grandfather were shepherds, and both singers and collectors of songs. Robbie showed me an old book with hundreds of songs written out in longhand by candle and paraffin lamplight over his fifty-five years as a shepherd. His conversation was punctuated by snatches of song, and every now and then he would pick up the old fiddle and rattle off a medley of tunes, some of them his own.

Robbie Murray started work at three shillings and fourpence a day, and after a week of long days on the hill, used to work until midday on Saturday, then walk nearly 10 kilometres across country to play football, and walk back home again. Looking at the frame of the man, I could well believe his stories of the rigours of his working life. Weatherman Stuart McSkimming told me that in days past, no one could match Robbie's great, long strides on the hill. McSkimming is a pretty hardy character himself, and when he's not padding the hills checking his rain gauges and making his weather reports, he's out walking long distances just for the joy of it. If Stuart McSkimming says Robbie was hardy, he was hardy.

Like many another, Robbie mourned the loss of the landscape he knew, and he told me it saddened him to look from his window and see his beloved hills smothered in forest. I asked him to look back on his life, and think about the things he'd like to have done. If the question was a stock one from the interviewer's repertoire, the answer was less standard. 'Och, I would have learned to read music, and I would have learned to ski.' When I raised my eyebrows at the idea of skiing, he told me that the hill he had herded caught a great deal of snow. 'With two feet on it, it would carry you, but when you lifted one, you'd sink to the thigh. Yon was hard work. The skis would have been right handy.'

LOCHINVAR AND MORE MARTYRS

L OCHINVAR COULD come as a disappointment to anyone who had Sir Walter Scott's *Marmion* drummed into them at school.

> *O young Lochinvar is come out of the west,*
> *Through all the wide border his steed was the best;*
> *And, save his good broadsword he weapons had none,*
> *He rode all unarm'd and he rode all alone.*
> *So faithful in love and so dauntless in war,*
> *There never was knight like the young Lochinvar.*

Not bad really, but being Glasgow weans, we had to improve it.

> *O young Lochinvar is come out of the west,*
> *His shirt tail hingin' oot, and a hole in his vest.*

The loch itself is not very exciting, but I was intrigued to see that a kestrel had chosen to nest in the garden of the only house to be seen, where it had appropriated an old crow's nest in a high tree.

Benbrack presents a considerable obstacle on the way, and at 580 metres is the second-highest point on the whole route (the Lowther

Lochinvar

29

Hills above Wanlockhead are the highest). This is a fine place in good weather, with splendid views in all directions, but in foul conditions it can be miserable, and in poor visibility, rather worrying. It is not a stretch to be taken lightly, and some walkers understandably choose to cheat, skirting round by the Water of Ken, and through the forest to Polskeoch.

I was looking for Allan's Cairn, another of the martyrs' monuments, when I came upon some really heavy work being done on the path. There was a mechanical digger at work, and countryside ranger Keith Kirk explained what was going on. This was a particularly bad stretch of the path, and digger driver Donald Millburn was skilfully slicing off the surface layer of heather and peat in great iron handfuls. This was placed to one side, and the underlying shale and rock dumped to make a ribbon of hard path. After the digger had flattened and solidified this, the peat and heather were replaced, leaving nothing more than a depression in the ground. The new path looked a bit unsightly, but Keith assured me that in no time the heather would creep up over the edges, and the path would become an acceptable part of the landscape.

Allan's Cairn stands at an open spot in the forest, and consists of a four-sided, capped obelisk standing about 1.5 metres high, the whole structure protected by a ring of iron railings. Every surface of the stone is inscribed with rather purplish prose which tells among other things that the stone is:

> *In memory of George Allan and Margaret Gracie*
> *Who followed Christ to martyrdom*
>
> *They were shot by the dragoons of Coupland and Lagg*
> *Near the Fawns of Altry in the days of the Covenant.*

As I approached the cairn I spotted a figure crouched in the steady drizzle, busily sketching. This turned out to be one Robin Ade, whom I knew from his books. Robin is a naturalist and wildlife artist who lives by the Water of Ken. He walks these hills regularly, and is much interested in the changes which have been, and are being, made in the area. He welcomes few of these changes, for the main effect has been the decimation of once thriving rural populations.

When Robin had taken his sketch as far as he needed, we walked together down the hill on the forestry road to the bothy at

30

Polskeoch. This is, by bothy standards, a de luxe model, built in 1986 by some of the lads of the army engineers, and kept in good order by a retired enthusiast who takes on running repairs and cleaning on a voluntary basis. It's a very useful bothy, not only to walkers but to the mistle thrush which built its nest about a metre from the ground, in a pile of cut logs. A strange choice, with hundreds of thousands of living trees all around.

SANQUHAR: A BUILDER, A KEEPER, AND A LESSON

THE APPROACH to Sanquhar runs close by a housing scheme and, though quite an attractive wee housing scheme, it's not quite what one wants on a long-distance cross-country walk. However, the housing scheme leads to Sanquhar Castle. The castle is very ancient, going back to the fourteenth century, though it has since been much altered and extended. William Douglas, first Duke of Queensberry, who built the awe-inspiring Drumlanrig Castle, also acquired Sanquhar Castle in the seventeenth century. He became so

Sanquhar post office

31

attached to the relatively modest Sanquhar that he chose to live there, spending almost no time at all in the opulence of Drumlanrig.

Many people know about Sanquhar Castle, but a lot more know about Sanquhar post office. It's a modest enough wee post office, though it does have an attractive bay window, but it just happens to be the oldest in Scotland, dating from 1763. The mail was delivered on horseback, and though it did take marginally longer than today, if the horse didn't blow a gasket it arrived pretty well when you were told it would. For its size, Sanquhar has quite a lot to offer – friendly people, for one thing. I was stopped a dozen times or so on my progress along the main street, which is very pleasant if you're not in a rush . . . and on a 340-kilometre walk, who rushes?

There's yet another Covenanting monument at the end of the main street; a rather large one in the form of an obelisk. It marks the spot where, in 1680, one Richard Cameron posted notice that he was not at all enamoured of the King, his government, and their outlandish religious notions. Needless to say, this was not well received, and despite being quick on his feet, Cameron did not last out the year. There is also a very handsome tollbooth designed by William Adam. No one, to my knowledge, posts notices on it, though they might like to, for, impressive as it is, the tollbooth is a considerable obstruction to modern traffic.

It was said of William Adam that he 'acquired a handsome fortune with an unspotted character'. Not an easy thing to do. The work of William Adam has long been overshadowed by that of his brilliant son Robert, who, with his younger brothers and two sisters, set about the task of revolutionising English domestic architecture. However, the achievements of the father have been re-examined of late, and his work very favourably reassessed. Though remembered as an architect, he was very much a lad o' money-making pairts, and was involved in coal, land, salt, bricks and tiles, forestry and agriculture, stone and marble, milling and brewing, and all aspects of civil engineering. William Adam's country houses – Mellerstain, Dun, Haddo, and many more – are acknowledged masterpieces, and it is the master's control, not only of the structure, but of the interior decor and the landscaping of the grounds, which gives these timeless buildings their clear, cohesive character.

The way out of Sanquhar is a pleasant one on a rising lane known as the Cow Wynd. The local people use this path for their evening

Kenny Houston

and weekend walks, and benches are strategically placed for the short-winded and shoogly-legged. I was very grateful.

There is a good stretch of open hill country and grouse moor between here and Wanlockhead, and it was on Glengaber Hill above the village that I had arranged to meet gamekeeper Kenny Houston, who works on the Buccleuch estate. Kenny struck me as being typical of his kind: a lean, quietly confident man, with the tough, spare kind of build which is ideal for covering long distances over rough ground. In tweed bunnet and breeks, he looked every inch the seasoned outdoor man he is.

Townies are sometimes puzzled by the patchwork appearance of grouse moors, and Kenny explained that this is because the heather is burned in patches, usually on a seven-year rota. The idea is to provide the grouse with heather at all stages of growth, from the young fresh growth for food, to high rank growth for cover and nesting. As Kenny pointed out, an area like this, wilderness to the untutored eye, is as carefully managed as farmland – the object being to produce the maximum number of healthy birds for the shooting season, which begins on 12 August and goes on late into the year. With people willing to pay substantial sums for shooting, the grouse are now crucial to the economic survival of many estates. Kenny Houston is a committed supporter of the system, and deplores the deterioration he sees in the countryside when an estate fails, or is badly managed.

During the grouse-shooting season and at lambing time, Kenny persuades people to detour and skirt the area, mainly for their own protection. We had quite a long conversation about wildlife, and I wondered if he felt, as I did, that there were fewer birds around. He

33

told me that he had noticed a very marked decline in the numbers of birds like curlew, lapwing, lark, wheatear, and even the ubiquitous meadow pipit. When I asked why, I was told that the increase in the numbers of protected birds of prey was a contributory factor, but that many people in the area felt that the Chernobyl disaster had had more effect than was officially acknowledged. Kenny also wryly pointed out that Windscale (Sellafield) is, relatively speaking, on his doorstep.

I was interested to compare my own amateur knowledge of wild-life with Kenny's day-to-day, on-the-ground experience. On the subject of hen harriers attacking people near their nests, I contended that all the swoops and dives, dramatic though they might be, were just bluff. Kenny quietly insisted that they would actually strike if pressed, and further along the route, I had reason to remember his words.

I had inadvertently strayed into the nesting territory of one of these spectacular predators, and could tell by the agitated behaviour of the hen bird that I was close to her nest. I attempted to retreat, but was obviously getting closer, rather than further away, and the rush of wind from the metre-wide wing span of the diving bird was getting positively alarming. The hen harrier carries a formidable armament of beak and claws, and I was perfectly happy to clear off and leave her in peace. The bird didn't quite understand, and when she finally did clout me on the back of my retreating head, she drew blood, and lifted a clump of my boyish curls. As I stumbled off, curs-ing and nursing my wounds, Kenny's words came back, and I thought, 'Don't argue with the man who knows.'

WANLOCKHEAD AND A DREAM BECOME REAL

A lonely wee toun,
Far hid among the hills o' heather sae broon*,
Wi' its hooses, reel rack†, keekin'‡ oot at ilk§ turn.

ROBERT REID's words make Wanlockhead seem quite attrac-tive, but my first sight of it as I descended the hill after leav-ing Kenny Houston was not at all appealing. Below me lay a

Wanlockhead beam engine

wide area of scarred industrial wasteland. This is a relic of the lead smelting which was carried out here in the mid-nineteenth century by the Duke of Buccleuch. The ore which was mined nearby was mixed with lime to aid the flow of molten lead, and with coal and peat as fuel, long wooden tunnels were led into the hill to dispose of the noxious fumes. The remains of the tunnels can still be seen. Where there is lead there is normally some silver, but Wanlockhead also had zinc, and even gold, making it a centre of mining since mediaeval times.

Mining of one kind or another went on until the Fifties when it came to an end, though, surprisingly, the village itself didn't die. In fact people are actually moving in here, a fair proportion of them English. This really is surprising, for Wanlockhead is very exposed, and at 425 metres above sea level is Scotland's highest village. (Much to the annoyance of Tomintoul, which thinks *it* is.) In winter it can be a difficult place, yet still it seems popular, the houses well painted, and the whole place appearing to be well looked after.

There is no doubt that it is the mining and its history which attracts people to this hill village, and features like the old beam engine create a great deal of interest. The engine is a massive piece of equipment which was used to extract water from the mine workings. The huge beam is mounted on a stone column, and works on a see-saw principle with two buckets. There is a working model in the

---

* *broon* = brown   † *reel rack* = topsy-turvy   ‡ *keekin'* = peeking, peering
§ *ilk* = each

superb mining museum nearby. The Wanlockhead beam engine is a scheduled industrial monument, and is being restored.

Probably the most interesting place in Wanlockhead is the Loch Nell mine, which started operations in 1710, and is open to visitors. I was taken on a conducted tour by a loquacious and well-informed Glaswegian known simply as J.J. J.J. insisted that, like all visitors, I should wear a hard hat, and we made our way through a shaft which forced us to bend double, and which eventually opened into a high, narrow, slanting cleft in the rock. The walls were slick with damp, and J.J. told me that in earlier times, before draining techniques were properly developed, men and boys would often be working knee or thigh deep in water. At the end of the tunnel, an illuminated tableau has been set up, to show life-sized models of miners at work, using primitive tools and lamps, and wearing eighteenth-century clothing.

Wanlockhead had a library set up for the miners as far back as 1756, and the neighbouring village of Leadhills had one fifteen years before that, the oldest public library in Britain. There's an argument here again, for some people say that the oldest library is at Strathpeffer in Fife. They say it a lot in Strathpeffer especially.

The present curator of the splendid mining museum is Richard Ellam, and it was he who showed me around most of the places of interest, but the man who initiated the whole project and brought this place to life is Geoff Downs Rose.

Geoff is from Derby, and used to work for the National Coal Board. He spent his holidays in Wanlockhead over a period of years, and when he decided to make his home here after retiring, he became deeply interested in the industrial and social history of the place. As his researches went on, he began to dream of making the village a kind of living industrial museum. Geoff told me that his imagination was fired by the knowledge that from this tiny and remote village came gold which was used in the crown jewels. He learned that a miner had to pan enough gold for a wedding ring before he could marry, and that Robert Burns's horse Pegasus had been shod at the old Wanlockhead smiddy, with a poem as a result. A great deal of research and determined hard work has made Geoff's dream reality, and he told me that he is now quite content to sit back and let others get on with it. I somehow doubt that.

Pegasus at Wanlockhead

With Pegasus upon a day
Apollo weary flying
(Through frosty hills the journey lay)
On foot the way was plying.

Poor slip-shod, giddy Pegasus
Was but a sorry walker;
To Vulcan then Apollo goes
To get a frosty caulker.

Obliging Vulcan fell to work,
Threw by his coat and bonnet,
And did Sol's business in a crack –
Sol paid him with a sonnet.

Ye Vulcan's sons of Wanlockhead,
Pity my sad disaster!
My Pegasus is poorly shod –
I'll pay you like my master.

Robert Burns

A HIGH POINT AND A
HALFWAY POINT

LOOKING BACK from the Lowther Hills, Wanlockhead begins
to look quite attractive, and as you gain more height, its near
neighbour Leadhills comes into view. The skyline of the
Lowthers is dominated by the gleaming giant golf-balls of the domes
of the civil aviation radar installation.

I must confess that I treated myself to a sit-down about three-
quarters of the way up this highest part of the Southern Upland Way,
and I was overtaken by three sunburned and weather-beaten walkers
of mature years. They were all English and their spokesman, a
strongly built individual from Marlborough, described himself and
his companions as 'fairly agile grandfathers'. They looked all right to
me, as they plodded steadily towards the skyline, but I was concerned to see that as they reached the radar station they seemed to be

37

turning left. However, they soon changed direction and headed off to the right.

I was keen to see inside the station, and had already made contact with public relations man Willie Cairns, who could not have been more helpful. The result was that when I performed my old trick of bashing on the door and making naïve enquiries, I was immediately welcomed in by Peter Mills. I was then treated to an extensive tour of the buildings while Peter attempted, with qualified success it must be said, to explain the technicalities of the operation. He told me that they do see quite a lot of way walkers, usually asking for water, as they get very dry on a hot day after the long pull up the hill. I was surprised to hear that they even have visitors in mid-winter. This is a very high and exposed place, and Peter Mills and his colleagues are often moved to compassion by the sight of pathetic, frozen faces peering in at the windows. Ian Johnston, who works at the British Telecom station a little higher up the hill, is amazed that people ever come near the place in winter. Winds of 160 kilometres per hour are common, and Ian has seen the massive steel masts bending before the blast. He told me that on one occasion, when the whole area was iced over, he stepped outside his door, whereupon he was immediately whipped up by the wind, and sent whirling across the compound like a drunken ice skater. He finished up crawling to shelter on all fours.

The highest point on the Southern Upland Way lies a little way below the summit of the Lowthers, at 710 metres. Leaving the area of the radar station, the way takes the shoulder of the hill above the Enterkin Pass. It was here that the Covenanters for once scored a point when they ambushed a troop of government dragoons and released their Covenanter prisoners. A sad and frustrated Bonnie Prince Charlie also passed this way after his retreat from Derby. The Prince was bitterly disappointed that his own officers had prevented him from marching on to London – he was not to know that he was heading inexorably towards the slaughter at Culloden.

On a clear day, there is an impressive view from the high point of the Lowthers, taking in places as far apart as the Lake District and the island of Arran. The Ettrick Hills, which mark the beginning of the real Border country, are to be seen beyond the Daer reservoir. This huge body of water, which supplies half of Lanarkshire's requirements, is contained by a dam and earthworks forty metres high and three-quarters of a kilometre long.

Stopping for a brew-up in Watermeetings Forest, and consulting my map, I realised that there was cause for celebration. I had reached the halfway mark, and with a mere 160 kilometres or so to go, I felt justified in adding to my tea the merest hint of a little something I carry in a discreet flask for just such momentous occasions. I was already picturing my triumphant arrival in Cockburnspath; the village wild with anticipation; massed pipe bands busily getting out of tune; the Red Arrows warming up for the flypast. Perhaps the Duke of Edinburgh . . .

I got to my feet and set off once more, a spring in my step, and a rollicking old Boy Scout song on my lips.

Not too far past the Daer reservoir, on the edge of the forest at Earshaig, there is a beautiful little artificial loch. Verged by grassy slopes scattered with deciduous trees and carpeted with daffodils, the place demands attention. The water is rich in aquatic plants, and I sat for a while watching hovering dragonflies gleaming in the sun, ruby red and cerulean blue shimmering and darting among water lilies and flag irises. Focusing below the reflective surface, I could see that the water was seething and black with tadpoles. Tadpoles begin their lives as vegetarians, but as they develop, become carnivorous, and when food is in short supply will quite cheerfully eat each other. There was a graphic illustration of this in the bloated floating carcase of a frog which was covered in greedily feeding tadpoles, and the gruesome idea came to me that they might well be dining on their Mammy. I'm glad I didn't know about things like that as a wee boy when I thought tadpoles were cute enough to be collected in jeely jaurs.

Further on, the walker will encounter a violent contrast to the peace and beauty at Earshaig, in the racket, clamour and frenzy of the A74 dual carriageway and the main Glasgow–London railway line – both of which have to be crossed.

MOFFAT: TOFFEE AND TUPS, SULPHUR AND CEMETERIES

A T MY time of life, a really good excuse is required to indulge a shameful taste for boiled sweets, and the town of Moffat provided me with the perfect one. Moffat toffees are deservedly famous, and it was in the spirit of dedicated research that I sampled them very thoroughly. With a satisfied smile revealing my rapidly disintegrating teeth, I made my way along Moffat's fine, wide main street. The street is dominated by the famous Moffat ram, an imposing sculpture which acknowledges the long-term importance of sheep farming to the local economy.

Moffat has a very fine museum, and on my first visit here I spoke to Jane Boyd, who was looking after the place. Jane chose to have our conversation, not in the museum, but in the cemetery – two cemeteries really, for as Jane explained, when the place filled up in the middle of the eighteenth century, they simply brought in more earth, and added another layer. The cemetery is well looked after, and has some very old, very interesting, and very huge stones. The famous road-builder John Loudon McAdam is buried here, and there is a monument to the driver of a mail coach who died in a snowstorm in 1840 while trying to save his passengers. All are overshadowed by an ostentatious structure reminding us of the great achievements of a local cattle-man in making piles of money for himself. The monument obviously cost a fortune; it's grandiose, vulgar and pretentious, and exactly the kind I'd like when I go.

Moffat was doing very nicely in a quiet sort of way, until a lady called Rachel Whitford discovered a mineral well just outside the town. It didn't make all that much difference for a while, but when improved roads made the town more accessible, a group of local wheeler dealers got together to form the Moffat Bath Company. They piped the water down from the spring, and built Bath Hall, with swish bathing apartments and assembly rooms. Bath Hall is now the town hall, but for a while it did a roaring, or gurgling, trade, and made Moffat famous as a spa town. It was the custom to take the waters at 7 a.m., whilst being entertained by the Moffat silver band. The horror of this situation was intensified by the fact that the mineral waters, in the tradition of all that is supposed to be beneficial, were thoroughly unpleasant, stinking sulphurously of rotten eggs.

Moffat's Black Bull Inn is of impressive antiquity. It dates from 1568, and has entertained, among others, Claverhouse, James Hogg, Walter Scott and Robert Burns. This is yet another hostelry where Burns scored his immortal lines on a window pane. This particular piece of hallowed vandalism is said to be preserved in the Soviet Union.

A FOREST OASIS AND A SCAR

AFTER FOLLOWING the Moffat Water out of the town, I soon found myself once again trudging through endless dark green forest. Just as I was becoming thoroughly bored by the sameness of it all, I came upon a sign directing me to a cottage where, it seemed, refreshment was to be had. This was like finding a pub in the Gobi Desert, and was not to be missed. Following the twisting path down through the trees, I found a beautifully kept little house with a few tables and chairs set outside, and chickens and goats wandering around. Over pots of tea and buttered scones, Joy Potter told me that she and her husband Dennis moved from England, and bought the place on the strength of an advertisement in *Exchange and Mart*. They have never regretted it. Joy is happy with her strangely situated tea room, her goats and chickens, and Dennis drives the support vehicle for Walk the Scottish Way, an organisation which provides guided hill walks.

Leaving this comfort corner in the green wilderness, I arrived eventually at one of the more dramatic landmarks of the route – Craigmichen Scar. I was brought to this place on my first visit by ranger Keith Miller, who pointed out the deep scree-sided gully to our left as we walked along the shoulder of the hill. Keith told me that the big peak towards the end of the gorge was called Capel Fell and was just over 675 metres high. On that side of the ravine, the face is bare rock and scree, and it's easy to see that erosion is taking its toll. On the other side, the walking is easy as you make towards Ettrick Head, though it would help to have one leg longer than the other.

On my more recent visit to Craigmichen Scar, I had the pleasure of the company of two old friends, musician Dougie McLean and his artist wife Jennifer, who had come along to try to pick up some of the atmosphere of this part of Scotland. Dougie enhanced the walk with the odd tune on his flute, and we discussed ideas about the music for the television series.

THE OLD MAN OF THE HILLS
AND A RARE SPECIES

FROM CRAIGMICHEN Scar I made my way to the bothy at Over Phawhope where I met Keith Robeson. Keith is one of a rare species in Scotland: a Scottish countryside ranger. The influx of English and other nationalities to Scotland, and the buying up of everything from village post offices to islands and huge estates, can be explained in general terms by the north–south economic divide, and the total lack of controls. An early-retiring couple can sell a bungalow in Sevenoaks and buy an estate in Scotland. The predominance of English people in all the notoriously underpaid outdoor jobs is more difficult to explain. I wondered if young Scots were simply not applying for these jobs, but was told that this is not the case. More likely explanations seem to be that the people responsible for the hiring are themselves English and, secondly, that English applicants seem to be more confident, and present themselves more effectively in interviews. Whatever the reasons, and at the risk of sounding chauvinistic, it was a pleasure, just for a change, to talk to a ranger with a Scottish accent.

At the bothy I also met Dennis Potter from Craigbeck Hope cottage, with his support vehicle, and a group I had met near Capel Fell. Their leader was Stewart Wilson, 'the old man of the hills', as he calls himself. A handsome, fit-looking man with a splendid white mane, he dropped out after a life in teaching, and now takes folk on these guided hill walks. He loves it, and is an entertaining and knowledgeable guide. I had my picture taken with some of the group, and some time later received a print with this letter.

Dear Jimmie,
    This is a compromising snap of you and my wife.
If you don't send me £5 000 000 by return, you will
have to keep her.
    What excitement will do to people when they meet
a celebrity!
    I wish you well with your future programmes.
            Yours Aye,
                Jack Boyd

'A compromising snap'

SCABCLEUCH AND THE LONE LAKE

PPROACHING ETTRICK on the road which runs parallel to the Ettrick Water, I had an unexpected treat as I watched some sheep being worked in an adjoining field. I had to pause and watch for a while, as I never cease to be amazed by the almost uncanny empathy between shepherd and dog: in this case, George Bell and his collies Tan and Teenie.

There is a choice to be made at this point, as the way takes off up the hill at Scabcleuch, while a little way ahead is the monument to James Hogg, the Ettrick shepherd. The monument is worth the slight detour, as is the old kirkyard where 'Jamie the Poeter' is buried.

The word *cleuch* will be encountered several times in this area, and it is used to describe a small, narrow, steep-sided glen or gully. The pull to the top of Scabcleuch is rewarded by the first view of St Mary's Loch. The waters of the loch are unusually clear, without the peaty staining commonly found in Scottish lochs and rivers, and there is a notable lack of vegetation around the shores. The explanation is that there are very few soluble minerals in the surrounding hills, and on still days the reflections on the surface of St Mary's Loch are diamond sharp. Sir Walter Scott noted the effect in *Marmion*.

Ettrick kirkyard

43

Oft in my mind such thoughts awake
By lone St Mary's silent lake;
Thou know'st it well, nor fen nor sedge
Pollute the pure lake's crystal edge;
Abrupt and sheer the mountains sink
At once upon the level brink,
And just a trace of silver sand
Marks where the water meets the land.

Lone St Mary's lake is not as silent as in Walter Scott's time, but it is still much appreciated by visitors, and by the members of the local sailing club. Kenneth and Irene Allison and their friends gave me a demonstration of their skills with sail, undisturbed, I'm glad to say, by power boats.

TIBBIE SHIEL AND A
STORY-TELLER

ST MARY'S Loch and the Loch of the Lowes were one in the past, but are now separated by a strip of land on which stands one of Scotland's most famous hostelries, Tibbie Shiel's Inn. Tibbie Shiel was a most remarkable woman who lived through the last quarter of the eighteenth century and most of the nineteenth, dying at the age of ninety-five. As a girl, Tibbie was a maidservant to the parents of the poet James Hogg when the family lived at Ettrick, and among the countless words which have been written about Hogg, Tibbie's are probably the best remembered: 'He was a gey sensible man, for a' the rubbish he wrote.'

Tibbie Shiel was married to a mole-catcher who died leaving her with six children to care for. She provided board and lodgings at what was then St Mary's cottage, and by application and force of personality, built it into a place frequented by Hogg, Sir Walter Scott, and the literati and characters of the time. There were great nights of music, stories and drink, and after one monumental carouse, Tibbie asked Hogg what he would like for breakfast, to be told, 'Och, Tibbie, just bring in the loch.' Now that is a real drinker's drouth.

I have always felt that the inn has never been given the attention it deserves as an historic place, and far too many casual and thoughtless

Dinghies on St Mary's loch

changes have been made, though the building and its surroundings are still very attractive indeed. Tibbie Shiel's Inn is now owned by a retired couple from Kent.

On a previous visit to the loch, I had met Tibbie's great-great-grandson Jim Mitchell, and it was good to renew the acquaintance. Jim is a sheep farmer who lives along the road, by the Megget Water, and he and his wife Doreen take a great interest in the traditions of the area. Doreen showed me some wonderful old visitors' books from the inn, and there were some letters too, including one from Tibbie to James Hogg. She asks Hogg's advice on the delicate matter of her son having impregnated a local girl, and the poet's simple recommendation is that they should marry and make the best of it.

Jim Mitchell is well acquainted with the work of Hogg, and is also keen on the poems of J. B. Selkirk, another local man. He recited for me, from memory and with great bravura, Selkirk's *A Border Burn* from the famous *Last Epistle tae Tammas*.

> *Ah, Tam! gie me a Border burn*
> *That canna rin withoot a turn,*
> *And wi' its bonnie babble fills*
> *The glens amang oor native hills.*
> *How men that ance have ken'd aboot it*
> *Can leeve their after lives withoot it,*
> *I canna tell, for day and nicht*
> *It comes unca'd for to my sicht.*
> *I see't this moment, plain as day,*

45

As it comes bickerin' o'er the brae
Between the clumps o' purple heather,
Glistenin' in the summer weather,
Syne divin' in below the grun',
Where, hidden frae the sicht and sun,
It gibbers like a deid man's ghost
That clamours for the licht it's lost,
Till oot again the loupin' limmer*
Comes dancin' doon through shine and shimmer
At headlong pace, till wi' a jaw†
It jumps the rocky waterfa',
And cuts sic cantrips in the air,
The picture-pentin' man's despair;
A rountree buss oot ower the tap o't‡,
A glassy pule§ tae kep** the lap o't,
While on the brink the blue harebell
Keeks o'er tae see its bonnie sel',
And sittin' chirpin' a' its lane
A watter-waggie oan a stane.
Ay, penter lad, thraw tae the wind
Your canvas, this is holy ground:
Wi' a' its highest airt achievin',
The picture's deid, and this is leevin'.

Jim Mitchell's head is full of poetry, stories and legends. He gave me a couple of lines which he had picked up somewhere and always remembered.

Sic a sicht as Sam'l saw,
Atween Dryhope and Tushielaw:
A big, big dug* wi' rid, rid een†,
Pu'in'‡ a coaffin oan a cheen§.

The dog is obviously the devil, and Jim would love to know the rest.

---

* *loupin' limmer* = leaping rascal   † *jaw* = to dash   ‡ *rountree buss oot ower the tap o't* = Rowan tree bush out over the top of it   § *pule* = pool   ** *kep* = keep

---

* *dug* = dog   † *een* = eyes   ‡ *pu'in'* = pulling   § *cheen* = chain

JAMIE THE POETER

Where the pools are bright and deep,
Where the grey trout lies asleep,
Up the river and o'er the lea,
That's the way for Billy and me.

HOW MANY generations of Scottish schoolboys learned the lines of *A Boy's Song*, and decided that perhaps poetry wasn't so bad after all? I remember with crystal clarity the effect it had on me: it seemed to depict the ideal life for a boy.

Where the blackbird sings the latest,
Where the hawthorn blooms the sweetest,
Where the nestlings plentiest be,
That's the way for Billy and me.

Where the mowers mow the cleanest,
Where the hay lies thick and greenest,
There to trace the homeward bee,
That's the way for Billy and me.

Where the poplar grows the smallest,
Where the old pine waves the tallest,
Pies and rooks know who are we,
That's the way for Billy and me.

Where the hazel bank is steepest,
Where the shadows fall the deepest,
There the clustering nuts fall free,
That's the way for Billy and me.

This I know I love to play,
Through the meadow among the hay,
Up the water and o'er the lea,
That's the way for Billy and me.

It was a long time before I learned that the writer James Hogg had lived just that kind of life as a lad: that he had become a cowherd, a shepherd, a fiddler and story-teller, and finally, one of Scotland's literary giants. James Hogg, the Ettrick Shepherd, was almost a caricatured example of the traditional Scottish self-educated man.

The
James Hogg
Monument

He had no schooling after the age of seven, but his empathy with the traditional songs, ballads and legends of the borders led him to learn to read and write. He devoured books, and by the age of thirty was thoroughly acquainted with the works of Shakespeare, the Scottish poets, Pope, Dryden, Smollett, Fielding and many others.

By the time Hogg went to Edinburgh at the age of thirty-nine he had a huge volume of his own writing behind him. His ballad collection, *The Queen's Wake*, made a great impression and, like Burns, he was fêted in the capital, as a rustic curiosity, but also as an obviously remarkable talent.

When Hogg married Margaret Phillips and settled to farm and write in Ettrick, he lived a life full of music, conversation and companionship, and happily combined a vigorous outdoor life with his literary pursuits. James Hogg was wary of the dangers of over-sophistication, and looked to sensuality, emotion and the power and resonance of the Scots language for his effects. He was a romantic, but at the same time a realist who warned against heroes, perfect people and perfect literature. He quite deliberately avoided self-conscious elegance, and said:

> *Most men will relish what is natural and simple if they are*
> *permitted to judge for themselves. If you take the most admired*
> *passages from the best authors, you will find them to be the natural*

48

expressions of men of good sense; and you will admire them, because you feel that they are precisely what you would have thought and said yourself on the same occasions; that they are, in fact, the things which have always been thought, but never so well expressed.

The apparent grammatical clumsiness of the title of one of Hogg's best-known songs, *When the kye comes hame*, demonstrates once again Hogg's rejection of pretence of any kind. He tells us:

I was once singing it at a wedding with great glee, When the kye come hame, when a tailor, scratching his head, said, 'It was a terrible affectit wy that!' I stood corrected, and have never sung it so again.

When the kye comes hame

Come all ye jolly shepherds that whistle through the glen,
I'll tell ye of a secret that courtiers dinna ken.
What is the greatest bliss that the tongue of man can name?
'Tis to woo a bonny lassie when the kye comes hame.

When the kye comes hame, when the kye comes hame,
'Tween the gloaming and the mirk when the kye comes hame.

'Tis not beneath the burgonet, nor yet beneath the crown,
'Tis not on couch of velvet, nor yet in bed of down –
'Tis beneath the spreading birch, in the dell without the name,
Wi' a bonny, bonny lassie, when the kye comes hame.

When the kye, etc.

See yon pawky shepherd, that lingers on the hill,
His ewes are in the fauld, and his lambs are lying still;
Yet he downa gang tae bed, for his heart is in a flame,
Tae meet his bonny lassie when the kye comes hame.

When the kye, etc.

Away wi' fame and fortune, what comfort can they gie?
And a' the arts that prey on man's life and liberty;
Gie me the highest joy that the heart o' man can frame,
My bonny, bonny lassie when the kye comes hame.

When the kye, etc.

A MISLAID YAK AND THE
RISING DEAD

THE WALK along the south shore of St Mary's Loch brought me to the farm at Bowerhope (pronounced Boorope) run by Mandi and Derek Hook, and as I had once interviewed Mandi on my radio programme, I called in. As is usual in this part of the country, I was made welcome, and found that, among other things, Mandi is a superb baker. She and Derek, with their two sons Ronnie and Sam, live happily in the quiet of Bowerhope, where they breed llamas. That's right. Llamas. They keep an all-male herd, and the females are at Moffat. This keeps the peace, and the stud male has a trip to Moffat when the occasion demands. They do very well on our Scottish hills, though they are not too keen on rain. They are also rather curious animals, and one followed a walker so far along the loch that it was lost, until Derek received a call asking if it was he who had mislaid a yak.

Derek and Mandi Hook are English, but have become very interested in the way of life and traditions around the loch. Their two sons were baptised in a blanket preaching ceremony at St Marie's Kirk, the Kirk o' the Lowes, on the other side of the loch. The

Derek Hook at
Bowerhope

At the Kirk o'
the Lowes

Hooks' boys bring the number of baptisms in the ancient kirk to a
grand total of three in a hundred years. I first heard about the blanket
preachings when I was brought here a few years ago by a keen local
amateur historian called Alex Cameron. What remains of the old
kirkyard lies within a dry stane enclosure about sixty metres above
the loch's north shore, and Alex told me that the old kirk lies buried
now, together with the stones and graves of Catholics, Presbyterians
and Episcopalians, going back over six hundred years. Every year,
on the fourth Sunday in July, a service is held in the open air at St
Marie's. The minister speaks from under a canopy, as did the blanket
preachers during the Covenanting times.

There is a well-known local story that over a hundred years ago a
tenant at Bowerhope across the loch saw the dead arising from their
graves, in the form of white, swaying, wraith-like figures. After a
night of terror in expectation of the day of judgement, daylight
revealed that a pedlar had hung his clothes to dry in the breeze.

Not far along on this side of the loch is the famous Gordon Arms
where Hogg and Sir Walter Scott met and parted for the last time.
The present owner of the Gordon Arms, Harry Mitchell, was busily
converting part of the premises to accommodate way walkers who
will pass this way as they come round the head of the loch. He

Sign on the Gordon Arms

showed me round, and I thought it all looked very promising. It's interesting that along the loch shore you are walking in the footsteps of Bonnie Prince Charlie, who came this way on his confident march south. The soutars o' Selkirk were persuaded to provide 2000 pairs of shoes for Charlie's men, and it's quite possible that had Charlie won, they might have been paid.

ECOLOGIST AT WORK

FOLLOWING AROUND the end of St Mary's Loch, a rising walk through the fields takes you on to a track leading past the sixteenth-century peel tower of Dryhope, before going on to Blackhouse. Dryhope was at one time the home of Auld Wat of Harden, an outrageous hooligan cattle reiver, from whom Sir Walter Scott proudly claimed descent. The Douglas castle of Blackhouse is in a ruinous, sorry state, and perhaps it's because we are so rich in history in Scotland that we can virtually ignore a place like this, which represents so much of our past. On this site lived Sir James Douglas, who fought with Bruce for Scottish independence. Blackhouse is thought to have been named after Sir James, who was known as the Black Douglas because of his dark skin.

One of the famous Border ballads, *The Douglas Tragedy*, tells the story of the ill-fated lovers Lady Margaret Douglas and Lord William. Lady Margaret's father and seven brothers, disapproving of the

match, pursued the couple, and in the ensuing battle all nine men were killed or died later of their wounds. Lady Margaret and Lord William are said to be buried in the kirkyard of St Mary's Kirk above St Mary's Loch.

At Blackhouse, I had arranged to meet Ronnie Rose, who is senior wildlife manager for Economic Forestry. Ronnie is very much a man of the Highland outdoor and sporting tradition. His grandfather was an expert stalker and ghillie on Queen Victoria's estate at Balmoral. He also played the fiddle and taught Scottish dancing to the sporting guests. Because of the difficulties of travel at that time, people spent long periods on the sporting estates, and the stalkers and ghillies often added the pipes, the fiddle or the accordion to their outdoor talents. The family tradition continued with Ronnie's father, who was a stalker during the reigns of Edward VII, George V and Edward VIII, and in 1938 became one of the first professional stalkers to join the Forestry Commission.

After serving an extensive apprenticeship, Ronnie and his brother were given the job of tackling deer problems for the Forestry Commission. Ronnie soon realised that no one cared very much about the

Ronnie Rose

future of the wildlife and how it was being affected by forestry. He became tired of the slaughter of deer as the only solution to the problems, and he resolved to make a proper study of their habits, to see if they could be controlled in any other way.

Ronnie has now been placed in charge of the management of an estate at Eskdalemuir, and has struck up a very positive and productive relationship with an owner who is committed to the concept of an estate where commercial forestry can be combined with sheep, game, and wildlife; managed in such a way that all benefit.

Ronnie Rose's approach is to understand how everything works, and having done that, to manipulate it intelligently. He gave me what he called a simple example. He had constructed an artificial loch to attract wildfowl. The loch was well planted, and was so successful that it attracted a healthy population of water voles. They, in turn, were so successful that they began to cause damage by burrowing in the banks. Some way up the glen, a pair of short-eared owls were in residence. At one time, they would have been shot out, as was everything with a hooked beak. However, Ronnie knew that owls liked to eat voles, and he also knew that they liked perching posts, so he supplied some. Over a period of time, the posts were moved gradually down the glen, and eventually into the territory of the water voles. Result – fewer voles, more stable banks, happy owls and a happy Ronnie. Examination of the owls' regurgitated pellets showed that their diet had swung from field voles to water voles.

The loch looks very pretty, and is an asset to the wildlife, but even here, Ronnie Rose has thought the whole thing through, for there is a very deep channel in the middle to allow helicopters to dip the huge water buckets they use to quench forest fires.

Ronnie's approach is to get to know and understand the area first of all – the soil, the weather, the topography, and the animal and plant life – and then to try to make it work to the advantage of the whole estate. In the fight against voles, which Ronnie says do as much damage to trees as roe deer, kestrel boxes were erected around the estate. Turf was considerately placed in the bottoms of the boxes. The kestrels ignored them. Ronnie gave some thought to their normal nesting sites, and threw a shovelful of stony shale into each box. In no time, several pairs of kestrels were feeding clutches of young on the troublesome voles.

Roe deer can do great damage to commercial forestry, not so

much by feeding as by territorial marking and antler rubbing. Ronnie's answer to that is to provide an alternative to the valuable commercial crop. He has found that the deer actually prefer alder and willow, and especially cotoneaster. Ronnie has found the planting of deciduous trees advantageous in other ways. The insects which inhabit the broadleaves attract populations of small birds, which in their turn provide food for the predators, diverting them from the game birds such as grouse and pheasant.

My day with Ronnie Rose was exciting and stimulating, but very frustrating too. The man's knowledge, gained over years of on-the-ground experience, of the intermeshing of all the elements of the ecology, is subtle and profound, and I felt that a month rather than a day in his company might have taught me something. However, the delights of Innerleithen and Traquair awaited me, and I left Ronnie Rose, determined to take up his invitation to return.

STEEKIT YETTS AND THE LAIRD'S ALE

I AM FORTUNATE in having visited many of Scotland's great houses and castles, and it's interesting to note which ones stick in the mind. Perhaps Dunrobin and Taymouth for sheer extravagance, Craigievar for its comfortable size and superb design, Eilean Donan for its situation, but Traquair House has to be my favourite. To begin with, it's a home. It's lived in and has always been lived in, and I think this gives the place a special feeling. It is also simply beautiful. The proportions are perfect, and the architectural details are just right. There aren't too many of them, and they always seem to occur at exactly the proper places on the old mellowed surfaces. The twentieth laird, Peter Maxwell Stuart, and his wife Flora obviously love the place, and are nice enough people to deserve it. Like many of the great houses, Traquair sustains itself in part by opening to the public, and it was Peter Maxwell Stuart's parents who carried out the repair and refurbishment which allowed the house and grounds to be opened in 1952.

I have twice been entertained at Traquair, and on the first occasion I made a point of arriving at the famous Bear Gates. The gates once opened on to the long drive which leads to the house, but on an

Traquair House

autumn day in 1745, the fifth Earl of Traquair said his farewells to the young Prince Charles Edward Stuart, with the promise that the gates would never again be opened until the Stuarts were restored to the throne. They have never opened, and are known as the Steekit Yetts, the closed gates. A great deal has been written about Traquair during its long history, including these lines by the poet W. H. Ogilvie:

Till the King returns

The wild rose twines on the gateway there,
The green weed grows and the bramble clings,
Barring the road to thy hearth, Traquair,
With the loyal hands of the earth's green things;

The wind through the rusted iron sings,
The sun on the self-sown tangle burns,
But never a hoof on the roadway rings –
The gate is shut till the King returns.

The Bear Gates, Traquair

I had a lover gallant and fair –
Ah! nought but sorrow the memory brings!
I opened my heart to him, everywhere.
He was my guest, and his right a King's.

But lightly his love at the last took wings,
Flying away with the hawks and herns,
And a gate no more on its hinges swings –
My heart is shut till my King returns.

The Stuarts of Traquair were Catholic and Jacobite and, like many another, paid dearly for it. Charles the fourth Earl, who married Lady Mary Maxwell, was sentenced to death and sent to the Tower, but he had married the right girl, for it was she who organised a successful escape. After the disastrous failure of the 1745 rebellion, the fifth Earl too went to the Tower, but with that delicacy of style displayed by the aristocracy when they're not murdering each other, the Earl's wife was allowed to stay with him, and they had a suite of three rooms for which they paid seven guineas.

For a long time after Culloden, the fortunes of the house were in decline. The estates had diminished, and the house which had once

entertained the grand and great of the country was quiet. As Peter Maxwell Stuart says, 'The family had simply taken the wrong side in religion and politics, and the house became a living symbol in stone of lost causes.'

Traquair is the oldest inhabited house in Scotland, and it's said that it began as a heather hut in the year 950. Since it was visited by Alexander I in the year 1107, the house has seen twenty-six kings, and it was here that Mary Queen of Scots nursed the son who was to become the first king of both Scotland and England. His ornate cradle is still preserved in the house, in perfect condition. The house has undergone many changes but it was in the seventeenth century that it changed from a fort to the splendid building we see today.

When Peter Maxwell Stuart was showing me around on my first visit, he took some pleasure in telling me, a Glaswegian, that Glasgow had been invented at Traquair. In 1175 King William the Lion signed a charter which granted a little village on the Molindinar burn the right to call itself a borough, and to hold a market day on Thursdays. That village is now Glasgow.

The history of Traquair House would fill a very large book, and another would be required to describe adequately its priceless contents. There are ancient embroideries and tapestries, some of them by Mary Queen of Scots; endless old manuscripts of great historic interest; silver, glass and pottery in abundance. There is the old

The cradle of James VI of Scotland and I of England at Traquair

Ian Cameron, brewer

58

library, and the secret room with its concealed stairway and escape route, where mass was said when the persecution of Catholics was at its worst. Traquair House and its magnificent grounds will repay visit after visit.

Hot food and good baking are to be found at the attractive tea room where Carol Farmer and her colleagues look after the visitors; though you may have to share your meal with some very bold peacocks, blackbirds, and a whole flock of incredibly tame chaffinches. Finally, you must not leave without sampling the famous Traquair ale from the eighteenth-century brewhouse. If I am any judge, brewer Ian Cameron has mastered his craft, though for seventeen years the ale was brewed by the laird himself.

The bush aboon* Traquair

Hear me, ye nymphs, and every swain,
I'll tell how Peggy grieves me;
Tho' thus I languish and complain,
Alas! she ne'er believes me.
My vows and sighs, like silent air,
Unheeded never move her,
The bonnie bush aboon Traquair
Was where I first did love her.

That day she smiled and made me glad,
No maid seem'd ever kinder,
I thought myself the luckiest lad,
So sweetly there to find her.
I tried to soothe my am'rous flame,
In words that I thought tender;
If more there pass'd I'm not to blame,
I went not to offend her.

Yet now she scornful flies the plain,
The fields we then frequented;
If e'er we meet she shows disdain,
And looks as ne'er acquainted.
The bonnie bush bloomed fair in May,
Its sweets I'll aye remember,
But now her frowns make it decay,
It fades as in December.

Ye rural Pow'rs who hear my strains,
Why thus should Peggy grieve me?
Oh! make her partner in my pains,
Then let her smiles relieve me.
If not, my love will turn despair,
My passion no more tender,
I'll leave the bush aboon Traquair,
To lonely wilds I'll wander.

Robert Crawford

TIBBIE CLOVENFOOT

A T INNERLEITHEN, I decided to stay at the Traquair Arms. It's an oddity in this part of Scotland in that it's not run by English people but by a Scottish couple, Marian and Hugh Anderson. Marian is a local girl, and Hugh is from Shetland. I enjoyed my stay at the Traquair Arms, not least because it is the centre for regular evenings of jollity, with folk music, monologues and poetry readings: echoes of the nights at Tibbie Shiel's with Hogg, Scott and their friends, and part of a living tradition in the

---

* *aboon = above*

60

Borders. Some of the music and poetry is fairly serious, but probably more typical is *Tale of a Sheep* from Howard Purdie. It is based, however loosely, on fact. Here is the official publicity hand-out for Mr Purdie's opus.

> *Tibbie Clovenfoot, the famous sheep of Howford Farm, Traquair, was born during the lambing season of 1988. It soon became clear that Tibbie was no ordinary lamb, refusing to eat grass or keep company with other sheep. Instead, she took a fancy to a local bard, Howard Purdie, who fed her with brown bread and cabbage sandwiches, and the occasional dram of Glenmorangie. It is no surprise, therefore, that Tibbie used to flee ower the dyke and trot doon the road at the heel of this bard, often joining him in cosy sessions in Ivy Cottage beside the log fire. Over a dram, bard and sheep mulled over many a plan to make the world a safer place for yowes and men. The bard wrote the following poem in praise of his friend:*

Tibbie Clovenfoot

Tho' Tibbie is the choicest lamb,
Mint sauce will never touch her.
A sad wee case when she was born,
A pechin', slaverin' creature,
Somehow she survived the storm
And syne she jouked* the butcher.

She should hae got a dunt† at birth
To dae the herd a favour;
But Jennifer, the fairmer's wife,
Had hert enough tae save her.
Then Uncle Howard sallied forth
And daily went and fed her.

As senseless as a Howford neep‡,
Still sookin' like a lemon,
She doesnae think she IS a sheep,
And doesnae want tae ken them.
She gars§ the herd and fairmer greet,
Her carcase winnae pey them.

---

* *jouked* = dodged   † *dunt* = a knock or blow   ‡ *neep* = turnip   § *gars* = makes

Her mummy lies in mutton pies,
Her sisters lie in pieces;
Shoulders, rumps and chopped-up thighs,
And aa withoot their fleeces.
Tibbie's the yin that's still alive:
The wonder never ceases.

She flits the meadows up and doon
For neither rhyme nor reason;
She dances tae her ane wee tune –
The Fairies find her pleasin'.
She serenades the sun and moon,
And bleats the comin' season.

Nou folk come frae near and far
Frae over there and yonder,
Tae gaze upon the Tweeddale Star
And speculate and ponder:
How this wee sheep aboon them aa
Became the Warld's Wonder.

Tibbie Clovenfoot enjoyed this panegyric, and, in return, she promised to give the bard her fleece at the next shearing. Unfortunately, this was not to be, for during some really chilly damp weather, wee Tibbie caught pneumonia and fell into a decline. Although the bard, with the help of local folk-singer Ron Murray, built her a howff to shelter her from the cauld winter blast, Tibbie passed away on Christmas Eve without opening her Christmas presents.

The bard, too, fell into a decline and, weeping into his ale in the Traquair Arms, he composed an obituary for The Peeblesshire News, The Times, The Scotsman *and other public prints:*

Obituary

Suddenly, on Christmas Eve, after a short illness (pneumonia), Tibbie Clovenfoot, pet lamb at Ivy Cottage, Howford.

Despite tender loving care, and broon breid and cabbage sandwiches dipped in Glen Morangie, Ms Clovenfoot departed to the other side wearing a green woolly scarf, a present from a well-wisher.

The simple burial ceremony, a mixture of Christian and Buddhist rites, was conducted by Howlet the cat and attended by the Heid Yowe Howford, the birds of the air, and Howard Purdie, writer in residence to the laird of Traquair.

> *Hark! the Herald Yowes do sing,*
> *Wee Tibbie noo is on the wing,*
> *Playin' a harp in pastures pure,*
> *And chowin' gress for evermore.*

Tibbie Clovenfoot is buried to the left of the tattie shed at Howford Farm. A simple wooden cross marks her grave. It is not true that her carcase was sold to the Traquair Arms for Sunday lunch.

A CHEESE WELL, MOUNTED POLICE, AND MUCKLE MOO'ED MEG

THE WAY up on to the Minch Muir is through a mature forest, but this soon takes you on a track which has been trodden by countless travellers since at least the thirteenth century. It led Edward I on his way to give the Scots a drubbing, and much later Sir Walter Scott's mother came this way by horse-drawn coach, en route for Peebles.

As the forest recedes, the track leads on to the open hill, and to an ancient stopping place known as the Cheese Well. The Cheese Well developed as a protection against the hazards of travel in earlier times: inclement weather, accident, and robbers. To gain the protection of the fairies, tiny pieces of cheese were thrown into the well. I wasn't sure whether a bit of a Mars bar would be an acceptable sub-

stitute or not, so I simply took my chances, and encountered nothing worse than teeming rain.

That did not seem to present any problems for the two mountain bikers I met on the hill. Mountain bikes are becoming ever more popular on the Scottish hills, and people certainly seem to get to the most unlikely places with them, pedalling up the most daunting gradients and hurtling down them at breakneck speed. I had assumed that my two bikers, Karen Pollock and Kenny McLean, were seasoned wheelers, but discovered that this was their very first day. They were clad in light gear, but were relentlessly cheery in the unceasing downpour. I learned that Karen has a degree in zoology, that she and Kenny are in the Greenock police, and that this was their idea of a jolly day out. It was Karen's anyway. I wasn't so sure about Kenny.

When the very first Scottish youth hostel opened in 1931 at Broadmeadows, the ceremonial group walked over the Minch Muir, and the ritual was repeated for the golden jubilee in 1981. The way drops down from the Minch Muir to the Yarrow Valley, where, at Newark, the Battle of Philliphaugh was fought between the Royalists and the Covenanters. Back at Traquair, Peter Maxwell Stuart had told me that when the Royalists were routed, the Covenanters demonstrated that they could be as brutal and sadistic as their persecutors. Royalist prisoners were forced into the walled yard at Newark, and slaughtered to a man. This was when the fleeing Montrose was turned away from the door of Traquair, the laird pretending to be absent.

The Cheese Well

Yarrow has one of the finest houses in the area, Bowhill, set in some of the most splendid woodland. Huge, stately, mature beeches dominate a wide variety of tree species, widely spaced to allow a rich undercover of shrubs of various kinds. Bowhill is part of the Buccleuch estate, and houses a well-known collection of paintings by artists such as Raeburn, Reynolds, Gainsborough; and the fine furnishings, silver and other treasures associated with the great houses.

Yarrow is rich in folklore and legend, and in the early days of the Scottish folk revival I cut my tonsils on songs like *Willie's Drooned in Yarrow* and *The Dowie Dens o' Yarrow*. There are endless traditional stories, grist to the mill of writer and poet. One of my favourites is the tale of Willie Scott and Muckle Moo'ed Meg. Sir Gideon Murray of Elibank had caught Willie red-handed in the act of stealing his cattle. Willie was given the choice of hanging or marrying Sir Gideon's rather ill-favoured daughter. The bungling rustler plumped instantly for the rope. The story is true, though in fact Willie did eventually marry Muckle Moo'ed Meg. They made a success of it too.

THREE BRETHREN AND A POOR
BUT HONEST FENCER

FROM A place called Broomy Law, the track rises along the fringe of the trees, and up and across to an impressive landmark known as the Three Brethren. These are massive cairns, I'd guess over three metres high, and they mark the place where the three districts of Yair, Selkirk Burgh and Philliphaugh meet. By the Three Brethren I met Walter Elliott, who describes himself as a poor but honest fencer.

I know Walter well enough to be aware that he is one of those people who have taken self-education to a level which sometimes makes formal learning seem rather silly. He is a keen observer of Border life, an unashamed Scotophile, a writer and poet, and more recently, a broadcaster. I have interviewed him on a couple of occasions on my daily radio programme, and he presented the programme twice during my absence while filming. Walter's knowledge of language (with a special concern for the Scots language) is

extensive, and he has had a lifelong interest in Border legend, history and folklore. When I asked him what he found especially interesting in the area, he surprised me by launching into a fanatically enthusiastic and knowledgeable discourse on the remains of the Roman fort of Trimontium, near Melrose, at the foot of the Eildon hills.

I could write several chapters about Walter Elliott, but I will content myself with offering two of his poems. The first reflects Walter's deep concern over the erosion of the vocabulary and idiom of the Border country, under the influence of incomers from the wealthier south. The second is based on one of the most famous of the Border ballads, *The Twa Corbies*. In Walter's poem, the corbies are lawyers. 'Oo' in the Border tongue means 'we'.

The Twae Corbies

As ah gaed* bye the Paddie Syke
Ah heard twae corbies 'hint a dyke†,
The yin did tae the tither say
'Whae shall oo gaun an' rook the day?'

'Ah ken a weedae‡ whae is greivin',
Her man was rich when he was leivin'.
Oo micht could leave her something smaa
Wi' a' due process o' the law.

'Or then there is a ferm ah ken
That's held in dispute bie twae men;
Wi' sic a healthy disputation
It's shair tae end in litigation.

The Three Brethren

'A poor but honest fencer'

'Sae, oo could puu it oot for days,
Pretendin' that oo're deidly faes
An' split the hale estate in fee
Wi' half for you an' half for me.

'Then, gin oo tak a little care
Oo'll maybe rype§ the Borders bare,
Aye makin' sure that oo keep plenty
Oo'll be joco‖ wi' a' the gentry.

'Then there's a man that ah ken weel
A pair but honest fencer chiel¶
Oo'll tak him doon tae his last plack**
An' strip the serk†† frae aff his back.'

Tho' mentally, ah'm no that slick
That reference jist did the trick
An' swiftly ah did tak in hand
Tae purify the Border land.

Ah took ma nibbie‡‡ bie its heid,
Loup't ower the dyke and cloured them deid
An' cover't them wi' fail an' faggots
An' left them there for honest maggots.

---

* *ah gaed* = I went   † *'hint a dyke* = behind a dyke (wall)   ‡ *weedae* = widow
§ *rype* = reap, strip, steal   ‖ *joco* = jovial, smug, chummy   ¶ *chiel* = person,
man, lad   ** *plack* = old coin (a small amount)   †† *serk* = shirt   ‡‡ *nibbie* =
walking stick, crook

The Border tongue

Ah mind awfy weel in ma younger days,
When the tongue they spoke on the Ettrick's braes
Or the Yarrae hills was sae crisp an' clear,
Gi'ed a lift tae the hert an' a joy tae the ear.

Noo in the valleys ye hear tongues o' Wales,
London, New York an' the Yorkshire dales.
The auld valley folk are aa wede awa*,
Ye scarcely can meet wi' a native at aa.

Ma guid Border Scots is considert uncouth
As folk try tae speak wi' a bool in their mooth.
Ah'll sin be a ghost in me ain native land,
An' speak in a tongue that few understand.

SELKIRK, AND A DAY WASTED

WALTER ELLIOTT's beloved Selkirk is not on the route, but is close and attractive enough to merit a visit. The town has a 'guid conceit o' itsel'' and the locals say, 'A day oot o' Selkirk is a day wasted.' Another popular belief is that it is 'better to be a lamp-post in Selkirk than the Provost o' Hawick'. The first time I heard Selkirk people saying these things, I thought they were joking.

Scottish explorer Mungo Park is remembered here, as he worked in Selkirk as a doctor. The Selkirk cobblers may or may not have been happy to make their 'donation' of 2000 pairs of shoes to Prince Charles Edward Stuart's Highlanders, but there is consolation in the fact that they have a song in their honour, *The Soutars o' Selkirk*. Selkirk shares with some of the other Border towns the custom of the common riding. The ceremony is said to be at least four hundred years old, and the men and women of the town ride around the marches – the borders of the burgh, including the climb to the Three Brethren, where Selkirk Burgh meets Yarrow and Philliphaugh. This is the event of the year, and each trade and profession has its own flag-bearer, the whole event being colourful, noisy and thor-

---

* *aa wede awa* = all taken or withered away

oughly enjoyable. The serious purpose is to commemorate the Battle of Flodden Field which took place in 1513, and in one day wiped out a substantial proportion of Scotland's nobility. Selkirk sent eighty men to the battle. One returned. That terrible day in Scotland's history is remembered in one of our great laments, *The flooers o' the forest*. The version given here is the older one, by Miss Jane Elliott.

The flooers o' the forest

I've heard them liltin' at the ewe milkin';
Lassies a-liltin' before dawn of day;
Noo there's a moanin' on ilka green loanin',*
The Flooers o' the Forest are a' wede away.

At bughts† in the mornin', nae blythe lads are scornin',
Lassies are lanely and dowie and wae‡;
Nae daffin', nae gabbin' but sighin' and sabbin';
Ilk ane lifts her leglin'§ and hies her away.

At e'en in the gloamin', nae swankies‖ are roamin',
'Bout stacks wi' the lassies at bogle¶ tae play;
But ilk maid sits drearie, lamenting her dearie,
The Flooers o' the Forest are a' wede away.

*At hairst**, at the shearin, nae youths noo are jeerin',*
Bandsters†† are runkled‡‡, and lyart§§ or grey;
At fair, or at preachin', nae wooin', nae fleechin',
The Flooers o' the Forest are a' wede away.

Dool for the order sent oor lads tae the Border,
The English for ance by guile wan the day;
The Flooers o' the Forest that fought aye the foremost,
The prime o' our land lie cauld in the clay.

We'll hae nae mair liltin' at the ewe milkin',
Women and bairns are heartless and wae;
Sighin' and moanin' on ilka green loanin',
The Flooers o' the Forest are a' wede away.

---

* *ilka green loanin'* = every green grassy lane   † *bughts* = sheep folds   ‡ *dowie and wae* = dull and sad   § *leglin'* = milk pail   ‖ *swankies* = smart young lads   ¶ *bogle* = ghost   ** *hairst* = harvest   †† *bandsters* = a person who ties sheaves of corn   ‡‡ *runkled* = wrinkled   §§ *lyart* = partly grey-haired

A DISPLACED PERSON, SOOR PLOOMS, AND BRAW LADS

COMING DOWN through the Yair Forest, I once again encountered one of the main problems of marked walkways: erosion, in this case in the form of a substantial stretch of the path which had been churned into clabber, glaur, thick, slippery, gurgling, clinging, oleaginous mud. I think that the problem here is that the base is clay, so that the drainage is poor and the concentration of many boots along this channel through the trees has turned the path into an almost impassable quagmire. Walkers have already been forced to create their own unofficial way through the trees, but this too will inevitably deteriorate.

As I emerged from the forest on to the metalled road, I was greeted by an excited falsetto chorus of Jack Russell terriers, with a baritone obligato from a couple of labradors in the roadside kennels. The owner came out to quell the racket, and I found myself in conversation with James Bruce, a tall, elderly man from the Western Isles, as foreign in these parts as someone from Tristan da Cunha. James had worked here as a gamekeeper for most of his long life, and he remembered the dense forest above us as open moorland, the home of grouse, curlew, pipit, lark and merlin.

A short walk along the road from James Bruce's house brings you to the elegant triple span of the Old Yair bridge over the River Tweed. Between here and Galashiels, there are good views of Selkirk and of the Eildon Hills, a prominent landmark much loved by Borderers. The Eildons, which at the proper time of year blaze with the bright yellow of whin and gorse, consist of three main peaks: Wester Hill, Mid Hill and Hill North, with the lesser bulk of Little Hill between Wester and Mid Hill. Sir Walter Scott said that from the Eildon Hills he could identify over forty places famous in poetry and in war.

Galashiels grew on wool, and on the water which provided the power for its mills. Things are not what they were in the tweed manufacturing industry, but Galashiels is still important, with an internationally known college of textile design and technology. I was shown around Anderson's Mill where they make everything from tartan to cashmere, but the overpowering racket of the huge looms soon drove me out. The town has a statue of a mounted Border

James Bruce

reiver, which I think is a wee bit like having a sculpture honouring Al Capone. I was more impressed by Sir Hugh Lorimer's clock tower, well known to architects. Every evening at eight o'clock, the clock chimes out the tune of *Braw, braw lads o' Gala Water*.

I was extremely fortunate in arriving in Galashiels on the occasion of the famous Braw Lads ceremony. As happens in the other Border towns, the place goes completely wild on this occasion, and there is an unrestrained festive atmosphere which affects everyone. The Galashiels ceremony is a relatively modern one, having begun only in 1930, but it follows the common riding tradition. There is an impressive crossing of the River Tweed early in the morning by hundreds of horses and riders, then out to Abbotsford (Sir Walter Scott's house) and around Gala Hill back to the town. The whole festival celebrates one of those bloody incidents in Border history when some of the local Braw Lads surprised and slaughtered a group of English raiders who were resting in a copse of wild plums. Gala people have been proudly known ever since as Soor Plooms. Pride is important in the Border towns and Gala has adopted as its own Robert Burns's song, *Braw, braw lads*.

71

Braw, braw lads

Braw, braw lads on Yarrow braes,
Ye wander through the blooming heather,
But Yarrow braes, nor Ettrick shaws*
Can match the lads o' Gala Water.
Braw, braw lads.

But there is ane, a secret ane,
Abune† them a' I lo'e him better;
And I'll be his and he'll be mine,
The bonnie lad o' Gala Water.
Braw, braw lads.

Although his Daddie was nae laird,
And though I hae nae mickle tocher‡;
Yet rich in kindness, truest love,
We'll tent oor flocks by Gala Water.
Braw, braw lads.

Above Abbotsford

Left The Braw Lads, Galashiels

> *It ne'er was wealth, it ne'er was wealth*
> *That coft§ contentment, peace or pleasure,*
> *The bands and bliss o' mutual love,*
> *O that's the warld's chiefest treasure.*
> *Braw, braw lads.*

ABBOTSFORD AND WATTIE

I T W A S arranged that I should visit Abbotsford, the magnificent home of Sir Walter Scott, and the present owner, Patricia Maxwell Scott, had decided that I should arrive by boat across the River Tweed, in the style of visitors in Scott's time. My boatman was Nigel Fell, the local ghillie, who knows more about this stretch of

---

* *shaws* = woods   † *abune* = above   ‡ *mickle tocher* = much dowry   § *coft* = bought

the river than anyone. He told me that the fishing that year had been pretty good; though whether fishing on private rivers is ever good enough to justify the considerable expense of the sport may be questionable. Nigel dropped me on a shingly beach, and a pleasant walk across some wide fields and through an archway in an ancient yew hedge took me to the splendid buildings of Abbotsford.

I had spoken to Mrs Maxwell Scott before, but at a distance. She was in the BBC studio of Radio Tweed in Selkirk, and I was seated at my console in the Glasgow studio. She proved to be as charming in person as she had been on radio, and she introduced me to her equally charming sister, Dame Jean.

After I had dutifully, and genuinely, admired the imposing exterior of the house, Mrs Maxwell Scott ushered me into the main hall. The effect of this first room is almost overpowering, crammed as it is from floor to ceiling with artifacts collected by Sir Walter, and reflecting his eclectic tastes. Almost the first thing to take my eye was a quite grotesque tusked skull mounted on a plaque, and I had to study it carefully before I realised that it was the skull of a walrus which had been mounted upside down. Mrs Maxwell Scott told me that the Duke of Edinburgh had identified it instantly. I was given an extensive tour of the library, the drawing room, the beautiful dining room, and the compact, book-lined study. This is where Scott, with prodigious energy, poured himself into the works which were to make him famous far beyond his native country. Mrs Maxwell Scott pointed out the various personal items in the study, including the beautifully crafted little secret drawer in his desk, and the stairway which led directly from study to bedchamber.

Sir Walter Scott was a phenomenal success in his own lifetime, and he bought his estate in 1811, when it was known as Cartyhole Farm. He renamed it Abbotsford, and commenced a building and landscaping programme which stretched even his resources. Two different architects were involved over a period of years, but there is no doubt that the character of Abbotsford was stamped on it by its owner. Sir Walter's habit was to rise at 5 a.m. and settle at his desk by 6 a.m. His output was staggering, but the demand was even greater, and the success allowed him to sustain his development of the ground and buildings.

Scott was suddenly swept from the crest of this seemingly endless rolling wave of success when the publishing company of Ballantyne

was declared bankrupt. Scott, who was financially involved, resolved that no one would suffer loss on his account, and he set to work to make good the loss. His determination and productivity were awesome, but the strain told, and he became ill, dying at the age of sixty-one in the year 1832.

The influence of Sir Walter Scott on the world's perception of Scotland has been lauded and it has been deplored. It cannot be ignored. In his lifetime and for about fifty years afterwards he was the most famous Scot – in Europe and America as well as in Britain. It has been claimed that he invented Scottish tourism, and that what the English 'Lake poets' did for the Lake District, Scott's novels did for Scotland. Places like Loch Lomond and the Trossachs became romantic Meccas for travellers, and new roads and inns had to be provided to cope with the swelling flood of visitors. His works were translated into all the European languages; publishers competed for his work; and such was his popularity in America that fast ships waited to rush his latest product across the Atlantic.

Scott was an overwhelming, all-time bestseller, but there is no doubt that his reputation faded badly with the end of the Victorian era. There now seems to be a reassessment of his work in literary circles, and if he will never again be regarded as he was in his own time, his place in serious literature now seems assured.

Sir Walter Scott wrote about Scotland as a land distinct and different, and whether or not you approve of how he did it, there's no doubt that the resurgence of awareness of Scottish identity is responsible, at least in part, for the reappraisal of work which, 150 years ago, entranced millions of people of all kinds, in many countries.

GASWORKS, A GARDEN, AND CARING PEOPLE

IN GALASHIELS, I stayed at the Buckholmburn Hotel, which is run by Squadron Leader Ron Scott and his wife Noreen, and it was here that I encountered one of those little unexpected touches of hospitality which leave a happy impression. I had gone for an after-dinner walk which ended in a rather undignified scramble through head-high vegetation, and down a hill which was much steeper than I had thought. As I arrived at the hotel door, scratched,

sweaty and thoroughly discombobulated, I was met by the Squadron Leader, a large glass of something nippy in one hand and a jug of iced water in the other. I have to say that I was impressed.

The way continues from the Abbots' ford from which Scott took the name for his house and estate, and arrives at the road bridge which joins Galashiels and Melrose. There is now some unattractive town walking by old gas and sewage works, though Melrose itself is both pleasant and interesting.

I was keen to visit the old walled Priorwood garden, having spoken about it on radio. The garden, which is run by the National Trust for Scotland, specialises in growing plants for drying, and has an orchard which illustrates the different types of apples grown through the ages. The fine motor museum was also a must for me, old cars being one of my passions, but obviously the showpiece of the town is Melrose Abbey.

Founded by King David I in 1136, the abbey has survived attack after attack, and has been rebuilt several times. What is left of the old gravestones, the ancient, mellowed stone of the cloisters, the flying buttresses and the huge, vaulted church itself, makes a most impressive monument to architectural skill and religious devotion.

The town also has a youth hostel, a famous rugby stadium (seven-a-side was invented here), and only a short distance away is the

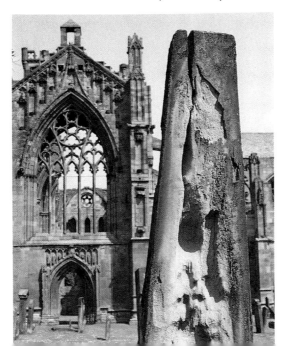

Melrose Abbey

The Tweed at Gattonside

Roman camp of Trimontium which so fascinated Walter Elliott.

The way out of Melrose is along the Tweed to a rather handsome old suspension bridge. Built in 1826, it has a wooden walkway, carried on two huge chains supported by finely proportioned stone towers. A notice informs us that the bridge is not to be used for horses, vehicles, cattle, etc. I'm not surprised, for it gets very bouncy and shoogly halfway across.

Not far from here, at Gattonside, I went to see a man called Brother Gregory, at St Aidan's, a centre which cares for the mentally handicapped. I had subconsciously expected to meet some kind of ethereal type in a long goonie, and it was a relief to find that Brother Gregory is a sturdy, affable man with a nice sense of humour. But Brother Gregory is not as ordinary as he looks, for, though not ordained, he has taken vows of chastity, and devotes his life to helping others.

The mentally handicapped used to be housed at St Aidan's, but are now dispersed throughout the communities of Selkirk, Galashiels and other Border towns. The buildings of St Aidan's are occupied by the Brothers, who run a busy industrial complex in Galashiels, producing such things as soft toys and furniture, and providing printing and graphics for local firms.

I was surprised to learn that the Brothers also own some fine fish-

ing on the Tweed, and that they allow fishing on Sundays. For many years fishing was one of the major recreations of the miners from the Edinburgh area. Sunday was the only day they had, and Brother Gregory said, 'Who are we to deny them the right to enjoy themselves?'

PRETTY LAUDER, LOUSY LAUDER, AND A FAIRY CASTLE

THE WALKER will once again encounter some fine, wide open walking country en route for Lauder, and especially on the Roman road which, though it rises and falls along the way, runs as straight as an arrow's flight, and provides firm, fast walking. Lauder is a typical little border town – clean, wide streets and low buildings giving an air of spaciousness. It has its common riding ceremony; it has a very striking little church with an octagonal bell tower; and it had the very first Covenanting martyr, the minister James Guthrie who was put to death in Edinburgh in 1661. There is the very inviting Black Bull, a one-time coaching inn, and nearby there is Thirlestane Castle.

Even in this land of castles, Thirlestane is quite extraordinary, a lavish extravagant fairytale of a building, and just what people expect a castle to be. The present owner has a name to match his castle: Captain the Honourable Gerald Maitland Carew. I found him enthusiastic, hospitable, and thoroughly likeable, though it appears that this description would not have fitted all of his forebears. On the road to the castle I had fallen into conversation with a farmer called Runciman, a friendly and talkative character who gave me a rhyme about the first Earl of Lauderdale.

Lousy Lauder cam' frae Leith,
Fower and twenty iron teeth;
Echt tae chack* and echt tae chow†,
And echt tae scart‡ his lousy pow§.

Much has changed since the time of the first Earl. The oldest part of the building with its circular towers – dozens of them, it seems –

---

* *chack* = click   †*chow* = chew   ‡ *scart* = scratch   § *pow* = head, forehead

dates from the sixteenth century, while the grand façade was developed in the seventeenth and the nineteenth centuries. Gerald Maitland Carew and his family occupy some of the ninety-eight rooms, but the castle and grounds are open to the public at certain times. Gerald told me that while he appreciates that he has a wonderful inheritance, he sees it as an enormous responsibility and a lifelong task. Among other problems, the central tower was in danger of falling through the building, and a trust fund has been set up to deal with restoration and maintenance. The laird showed me around as much of the interior as time would allow, and I was most impressed by his knowledge, and by his commitment to getting everything done properly without vulgarising the place.

There is a long stretch of open country to be traversed now, after passing the farm at Wanton Walls, with the mass of the Lammermuir Hills looming ahead. Two tiny cairns are just visible at the end of what appears to be a long ridge. After a good deal of slogging, these prove to be two massive columns, of dry stane construction. Each cairn has a recess which has given shelter to many a traveller. They are said to commemorate two young men who were sent out as champions to do battle for their respective armies. The story is told in the ballad *The Battle of Twinlaw* that they fought to the death, not knowing that they were brothers who had been separated in infancy.

> *And they biggit twa cairns on the heather,*
> *They biggit them round and high;*
> *And they stand on the Twinlaw Hill*
> *Where they twa brithers lie.*

TO MARK OR NOT TO MARK

I WAS ACCOMPANIED on the last stretch of the walk up to Twinlaw Cairns by Roger Carr, the energetic and personable chairman of the Countryside Commission for Scotland. As we relaxed at the summit on a sunny but boisterously breezy day, Roger had some points to make about marked walkways in the Scottish countryside. He told me that the three walks initiated by the Commission, the West Highland Way, the Speyside Way and the

With Roger Carr at Twinlaw Cairns

Southern Upland Way, had exceeded their most optimistic expectations; the West Highland Way being especially popular.

I put to him the worries and criticisms of many outdoor people: among other things, the intrusion of signboards and way markers and, more seriously, the erosion caused by too many people being channelled into too small an area. Roger accepted that these were real problems, of which the Countryside Commission were fully aware, but the situation was being continually monitored, and ways were being found to tackle the erosion. I worried that the solutions – duck boarding, gravel paths, hand rails and so on – were perhaps as bad as the problem itself.

Roger Carr is well aware that the situation has to be tackled sensitively and subtly, but makes the general point that the advantages of the walks far outweigh any disadvantages. Marked walkways were giving thousands of people the opportunity to become acquainted with their own country. The hope was that, having been introduced to the outdoors, they would derive a lifetime of benefit from it, and learn concern for the environment into the bargain.

AS ITHERS SEE US, WHITCHESTER
AND LONGFORMACUS

O N THE walk down from Twinlaw over the grouse moors I was treated to the unexpected sight of sheep being herded by motorbike. Very sensible, too, as the little cross-country bikes cope very well with the terrain, and can keep up with sheep and dogs, saving greatly on time. Even stranger was my meeting in Roughside Forest with Ronnie Dale and his go-anywhere Land Rover. Ronnie is a young local farmer and contractor who has developed a school for off-the-road driving. He teaches forestry workers, estate owners, explorers and the like – anyone, in fact, who wishes to take a vehicle where any sensible person wouldn't. He took me for a short drive on a part of the forest road, and though the vehicle seemed to be standing on its bonnet on some of the gradients, I felt quite relaxed, as one does in the company of someone who knows what he's about.

It was while Ronnie Dale was being filmed that I was interviewed by a young girl who was a part-time reporter for the local newspaper. Filming can be a tedious and repetitive business, and I could well understand that after asking a few desultory questions, she left us to it. I was rather surprised some time later to be sent a copy of her article, in which I was described as something resembling Dopey in *Snow White and the Seven Dwarfs*, Yul Brynner, and Quasimodo on an off night: 'A wee Glasgow blether, with not much hair and an expanding waistline.' She clearly did not wait long enough to notice the striking resemblance to Paul Newman.

Near the village of Longformacus, I stayed at an interesting place called Whitchester. Whitchester lies prettily in the foothills of the Lammermuirs, and is a beautiful old building set in well-laid-out grounds with mature, exotic trees and shrubs. My stay there was most relaxing and comfortable, thanks to the kindly ministrations of David and Doreen Mayberry who run the place as a Christian guest house and conference centre. Meals are superbly presented by Doreen, whose cooking has won her a Taste of Scotland recommendation. The whole atmosphere of the place is homely and comforting, with log fires, country walks, a very marked absence of piped music, and milky drinks at bedtime. Wonderful stuff.

Longformacus village is divided by a rather stylish single-span

stone bridge high above the river. When I crossed it I chatted to some wee village boys, who, with that casual disregard for safety which shortens mothers' lives, were dangling legs and fishing rods over the parapet. When one of them dropped line, rod and all into the water, he promptly raced home, got his trunks, and dived underwater to retrieve it. Longformacus is an attractive village though, like so many other places in the south of Scotland, incomers are making changes in the social structure and character. It has a shop, a post office, and a church which was founded in 1234.

ABBEY ST BATHANS: CHANGE, PERMANENCE AND POTS

THE ELEVEN kilometress or so of countryside between Longformacus and Abbey St Bathans are pleasantly varied, and you'll notice the jet black Welsh cattle which are a feature of the area. There was some kind of religious settlement at Abbey St Bathans in the Dark Ages, and much later a Cistercian priory, but there is no evidence of there ever having been an abbey. I walked along to the cosy little youth hostel and signed the visitors' book, before having a look around the trout farm and the compact visitors' centre, with Susan Millard's murals depicting life in the area through the ages.

In the square of cottages by the river, I met a lady called Mrs Todhunter who lived nearby at Shannabank Farm before moving into the village. Mrs Todhunter has seen much change, the main one being the influx of people from the south. She told me that she missed the noise and laughter of children in the village, and regretted the loss of the van which used to come round with groceries and confectionery. These were comments which I heard over and over throughout my journey, but like many older people, Mrs Todhunter was cheerfully philosophical.

A few metres from Mrs Todhunter's front door, a bridge crosses the river to a wood which has been designated a site of special scientific interest (SSSI). The reasons for this were explained to me by Chris Badenoch, who was the Nature Conservancy Council's representative in the area. Chris explained that the wood is interesting and important simply because it's old. There is very little natural,

unmanaged woodland left in Scotland, but the Abbey St Bathans woods are charted as far back as the sixteenth century. Chris looks for other evidence too. There are flightless beetles here which could only have arrived when the whole area was wooded. The ridiculous alternative is that they crawled more than 32 kilometres from the nearest similar wood. There is also the presence of plants like Dog's Mercury and Mountain Veronica which are found in old established woodland.

The basis of the whole woodland ecology is in the rotting timber, which is anathema to the commercial forester. Chris Badenoch pulled back a chunk of decaying bark from a fallen log, to reveal the white tendrils of the fungi which were breaking it down. There was a scatter of the various creepy-crawlies which are at the lower end of the food chain that ultimately sustains the birds and animals of the forest. An oak tree is said to play host to between 200 and 300 living things, and it can even withstand the onslaught of a certain type of caterpillar which completely strips the foliage. The oak simply waits until the caterpillar has done its worst, and produces a whole new crop of leaves. This is known as the Lammas growth, Lammas being the festival of fruits on 1 August.

The value of undisturbed old habitats like the Abbey St Bathans wood is evident in the fact that it supports twenty mammal species, and that 155 different types of bird have been recorded in or around the wood, together with reptiles and countless plants, insects, fungi, moths and butterflies.

The estate here is owned by the Dobie family. Mrs Helen Dobie inherited it, and her son Willie is now manager. I spoke to them at the big house, and Mrs Dobie remembered it as a magical place when she was a child. Things are more real now, and all the component parts of the estate must work as a commercially viable entity: the farm, the forestry, the sawmill, the trout farm, all playing their part.

Before leaving the village, I crossed the river by the ford to visit the pottery run by Carol Buchan and Peter Lochead, graduates of the Aberdeen School of Art. On leaving art school, Carol and Peter were looking for a country pottery, and were delighted when Mrs Dobie offered them this lovely situation. They are very happy with progress so far, Peter producing the ware, and Carol taking on the painting and decorating. As I used to be a potter, I had to try my hand on the wheel. I discovered that it's not quite like riding a bike.

Pease Dean

A BIG BRIDGE AND
A LITTLE DRAMA

A S I WALKED up past Shannabank where Mrs Todhunter used to live, I could understand why she had spoken so fondly of the place, but I was not so happy a little farther on when I realised that I had to cross the A1 with its racing cars and thundering juggernauts. To add to the rackety horrors, the railway line runs close to the road at this point. There used to be a tunnel here which proved too narrow for modern rail traffic, but an attempt to enlarge it came to grief when it collapsed, killing two men.

The walk through Penmanshiel wood ends suddenly with your first sight of the sea since Portpatrick – a view marred by the ugly bulk of Torness, though the Bass Rock can be seen beyond it. The deep gully of Pease Dean is the latest official reserve of the Scottish Wildlife Trust, and is spanned by a bridge built in 1783, which was said at the time to be the highest stone bridge in Europe. This is easy to believe as you look down to the burn about thirty-six metres below.

84

The Pease Dean reserve is not very extensive, but it includes a wildly overgrown glen with a profusion of plant life and attendant birds, mammals and insects. I am very fond of the story of Robert the Bruce in this area. It was here that he received a letter from the Pope and returned it unopened because it was not properly addressed to him as King of Scotland.

Not far from where you emerge from the nature reserve, and close to the end of your trek, there is the rather depressing spectacle of one of those huge caravan sites with regimented rows of vans crammed together, filling the bay, and with no attempt at landscaping or planting. Caravans provide a great many people with relatively inexpensive and enjoyable holidays, but surely they don't have to destroy the scenery which attracts people in the first place.

Strangely enough it was on the very edge of this eyesore that I was witness to a little wildlife drama involving a family of reed warblers. I had been watching the little birds darting around and calling with frantic excitement, and had wondered what was alarming them. The answer presented itself in the form of a russet-coloured snake-like head raised above the grass, tiny black bead eyes fixed on the flustered birds. A stoat on the hunt.

He darted with astounding speed and agility up into bush after bush, systematically hunting, probably for nests, with every move marked by the reed warblers. I was alarmed at how close the birds came to this ferocious little predator, and waited for the pounce which would put a bloody end to the hunt; but eventually the killer seemed to lose interest, and as he disappeared into the undergrowth, the panicky calls of the birds faded, and all returned to normal.

A SHORT LOOK FORWARD AND A LONG LOOK BACK

THE MOST exciting thing about this last stretch of the walk is that it *is* the last stretch. However, with only a few kilometres to go, there are still some points of interest. There is the much-reduced ruin of Fast Castle on a promontory high above the sea. The castle was a proud place of strategic importance in the fifteenth century, and commanded a tremendous vista of shoreline and sea. The nature reserve at St Abbs is an overpowering visual and

aural experience, and the smell from the hosts of sea birds on the cliffs is pretty overpowering too. Visit too late in the season, however, and you will be disappointed, as most of the birds come to the cliffs only to nest. As soon as the breeding season is over, they move back out to sea where they spend most of their lives.

Cove harbour seems to be chiselled out of the red sandstone, and there is an access tunnel through the rock to the bay. The tunnel is sixty metres long, and was cut in the middle of the eighteenth century. From Cove the way turns inland a little way to Cockburnspath, and the end of the 340-kilometre journey. Even here, at the old Mercat Cross, we are reminded of history, as the monument commemorates the marriage of King James IV of Scotland to the King of England's daughter, Margaret Tudor. This is the union which I saw celebrated as part of the Braw Lads ceremony, away back in Galashiels.

Looking back along the way, I seem to remember that there were too many dark green forests; too many noisy, low-flying aeroplanes; and perhaps too many hotels, craft shops, guest houses, post offices and dwelling houses occupied by non-Scots. These niggles fade to insignificance with the memories of wonderful, exhilarating countryside with its rich wildlife; fascinating history and legend, song and story; great houses and castles, and – most vivid of all – interesting, warm and friendly people.

At Cockburnspath